The Star at the End of the River

T0194225

The Star
at the End of the River

MEDITATIONS ON A HOMEWARD JOURNEY

PAUL VINCENT

iUniverse, Inc.
Bloomington

The Star at the End of the River
Meditations on a Homeward Journey

iUniverse books may be ordered through booksellers or by contacting:

iUniverse
1663 Liberty Drive
Bloomington, IN 47403
www.iuniverse.com
1-800-Authors (1-800-288-4677)

ISBN: 978-1-4502-8242-0 (sc)
ISBN: 978-1-4502-8243-7 (ebk)

Library of Congress Control Number: 2011900019

Printed in the United States of America

iUniverse rev. date: 03/21/2011

FOR CATHY

Beloved co-journeyer

TABLE OF CONTENTS

ACKNOWLEDGMENTS

I have never done this before—written a short memorandum of acknowledgment, that is. I have read many, of course; and what surprises me the most is how few offer thanks to that mysterious Presence that inspires people to do anything at all, at whatever index of quality. To that One, then, I offer my first gesture of gratitude. Next I must mention those whom I haven't the space to identify specifically: ancestors, friends at various times of my life, neighbors, work colleagues, and fellow communicants in parishes to which I have belonged. I am grateful for the contribution of all of these souls to my life's journey.

As regards those whom I want to name, I must first mention my sister Barbara. The simple fact is that this book would not have been written without her constant urging. For as long as I can remember, she has advised me to write down my ideas; now that I have done so, I render her my heartfelt thanks. Her husband Norm, a faithful conversation partner, also gave continual encouragement. My cousin Jan, her husband Norman, their children and grandchildren many times expressed interest in my progress. Finally, my wife Cathy's family—twelve siblings; over thirty nieces and nephews (some of whom have been overnight guests in our house); and a wonderful mother-in-law—have gifted me in ways hard to express in words.

I wish to thank specifically the following persons—dear friends and fellow seekers—who read parts of the manuscript and offered enthusiasm and helpful criticism: William Bourdeau, Gary Farias, Sue Kent, and Valerie and Henry Nash. I am also indebted to my spiritual director, Sister Virginia Sampson, for her interest in the project. A word of thanks is in order to Professors John Lawless and Patrick Reid of Providence College for their aid with some Latinisms about which I needed clarification. I am deeply grateful to Gary Farias, a multi-talented artist, who drew the two splendid diagrams in chapter nine. And I would be remiss if I failed to cite with thanksgiving the assistance and, above all, the patience of the staffers at iUniverse, publishers of this book.

Lastly, I name my loyal partner in life, Cathy, who has helped in this project in more ways than I can name. I dedicate this book—and all my moments—to her.

Bristol, Rhode Island
March 2, 2010

(1)

THE MEDIOCRE MYSTIC

"Happy the pilgrims inspired by you with courage to make the ascents."

Psalm 84 (New Jerusalem Bible)

For some reason, on the way to a church supper a few years ago, I blurted out to my wife Cathy that I thought I was a mystic, just "not a very good one." I'm not even sure what I meant—perhaps that my only random attention to things spiritual, and meager "results," compared poorly when measured against such titans of the art as Jesus, the Buddha, and St. John of the Cross. But I already knew that my statement ran counter to the advice of so many mentors, who counseled against such comparisons and self-evaluations as being gratuitous and, in the end, unhealthy. Better to have said simply (another evaluation!) that I felt drawn to the mystical life—which I did, and do.

But what exactly is it that I am I drawn to? Among the definitions of mysticism to be found in my modest library on the subject are the following: "a stretching out of the soul into God through unifying love"; "an intuition that transcends the temporal categories of the understanding"; or simply "union with reality." Bede Griffiths, in his remarkable book *The Marriage of East and West*, sums up these descriptions nicely in his discussion of the Hindu doctrine of non-duality, which describes a faculty deep within all human beings by which they are moved to oneness with the "source of cosmic unity" through an "immediate experience." For me, the mystical life has always included the sense that reality had a generous thickness perpendicular to, or athwart, the merciless drumbeat succession of moments that often dominates our life awareness. I realize in retrospect and with humility that on a number of occasions I have been allowed to enter into the "blessed thickness," this book being a partial record of such experiences. So, harking back to the conversation with my wife, I have dropped the self-description of "not very good mystic" and have settled instead on a designation of "mediocre mystic," which will strike some as not much better.

"Mediocre" is nothing less than a despised adjective, a label everywhere and always to be avoided. Over the years, its connotation of "less than desirable quality" has grown like a barnacle over what the word actually denotes: "of the middle," "ordinary." The application of the term to one's general spiritual life seems dubious, to the deeper mystical life, even more problematic. And yet, at second glance at least, the ordinary is not at all out of place in the sphere of religion.

Shunryu Suzuki, the great teacher of Zen, has described the practice of meditation as "nothing special," meaning that, properly understood, it is nothing more nor less than life itself—an odd notion when one reflects that the object of such meditation is to achieve union with "reality," "the divine," or "the timeless." But then we have Jesus telling his listeners in the Sermon on the Mount that life is more than food, the body more than clothing, coaxing them, in effect, to become mystics—this, to people who did not have enough to eat, only the clothes on their backs and therefore, of necessity, primarily concerned with the here and now. The inescapable conclusion? Mysticism is the proper business of all humankind, or, with apologies to Aristotle, "man is a mystical animal." If so, not the least of the outrages suffered by the desperately poor of this world is that the unjust conditions that they endure prevent them in the overwhelming number of cases from embarking on the mystical journey, which is their fundamental calling as human beings.

If all human beings are mystics, most must be mystics of the middle, mystics of the ordinary, mediocre mystics, I aver. The history of mystical experience is replete with theophanies, stigmata, wrestlings with angels, beatific visions—in short, "somethings special." I make no adverse comment on these singular happenings, and indeed own as not the least of my beliefs that the "God of surprises" is joyfully active in our world and universe, leaving His luminous footprints in out-of-the-way places and touching people with holy magic. But centuries of human experience have shown that for most of us, most of the time, it is not so. We, the happy company of mediocre mystics, must find the way in via the "nothing special" of everyday living in all its ordinariness. My own faith community, Catholic Christianity, which has at its center a very special divine intervention into human affairs, nevertheless recognizes this by designating over half of its celebratory year as "ordinary time."

Lately I've been thinking that, if the mystic of special revelation is expecting an angel, the mediocre mystic would do better to contemplate an angle. For the former, entrance into mystical experience is more nearly at right angles to the time stream, interrupting the flow; for the latter, it is at an acute angle, never that far from the actual experiences themselves. It is here too, that, seeing the mystical life under a different, but time-honored metaphor, the word "mediocre" can be of further service.

The suffix of "mediocre" is from the Old Latin, and before that, Greek, meaning "hill" or "mountain" (*ocris, okris/akros*, as in *Acro*polis). Etymologically speaking, "mediocre" means "halfway up a mountain." I find this interesting because a historically favored figure for the mystical journey is the climbing of a mountain—Mount Tabor, Mount Sinai and, not least, Mount Carmel, being three venues appropriated metaphorically by ascetic theologians and spiritual writers of the Judaeo-Christian tradition. One can see why the image has been irresistible, based on certain assumptions about human life, namely, that the path to the divine is a constant struggle "up" against the "gravity of sensuality" and all that is summed up in the concept of "the flesh." The earnest pilgrim is pictured here negotiating the path of perfection at a daunting, nearly right angle of ascent and within a landscape of apparent barrenness, fearful crags, and major catastrophes of backsliding. In this theater of understanding, "mediocre mysticism," satisfied with a halfway-up journey, could only be deemed a failure of the spirit.

But what if we were to see that the mediocre mystic ascends not halfway up a mountain, but up a "halfway mountain"? The image of such a mountain first broke through to me when I was examining my niece Abby's middle school general science text. There, in a section entitled "Using Simple Machines," I saw next to the pulley, the lever, and the wheel and axle a picture of the mountain of middle mysticism: the inclined plane! Here again is the acute angle of entry into the heavenly precinct, but conceived now as an angle of ascent—the slowly rising path, so convenient for transferring crates in warehouses and finding God along a manageable slope.

It was the way of the tribe of Judah returning from exile in Babylon and of all Jewish festival pilgrims as they joyfully sang their songs of ascent to Jerusalem, memorialized in Psalms 120–134. These are the so-called "gradual psalms," hymn-prayers whose very name describes the way of the mediocre mystic, ascending to the divine presence by slow degrees; journeying, sometimes haltingly, up the inclined plane. And if scaling the steep mountain of traditional mysticism requires courage, so too does the gradual upward climb: a courage to persevere in the search for the divine in the nearness of routine and in the predictability of the events of an average life.

This book is one man's "gradual," a song of an unremarkable ascent. It is filled with the media through which I have experienced the touch of God, alongside the ritual celebrations of my own religious community: words, music, and ideas;

people I have known; places that have spoken to me; events charged with heavenly resonance; hobbies and avocations—chief among them, night sky observing, every aspect of which for me has a divine nimbus.

I venture that there are no new ideas to be found within these pages. Why, then, even bother putting pen to paper or, rather, fingers to keyboard? Because, although this is a book about what, at bottom, I believe everybody knows, it is at the same time a record no one else could write. Every person who ever was born has a divine music within them—a song of the personal ascent. Why else were individuals created but to do this irreplaceable singing for others to hear? And, if it is not a book, then something else—whatever God has given. But to sing at all costs is the human vocation, even if off-key, and to ascend, ever homeward, the inclined plane.

(II)

DARK RUN

"I turn away, turn to the holy, inexpressible mysterious night."

Novalis, *Hymns to the Night*

"Night holds no terrors for me."

Antiphon for Psalm 91, Compline

I could feel pressure on my right forearm, but it wasn't an affectionate squeeze. I knew it was Cathy, who was sitting right next to me; it was obvious that she was grasping my wrist to alert me about something. As I leaned over to find out what was wrong, she was already whispering in my ear: "You're grimacing!"

I was. We were at Sunday Mass, and the lector had just completed proclaiming the second reading for the thirty-third Sunday in Ordinary Time, taken from the first letter of Paul to the Thessalonians. The offending line, which made my face a study in unpleasantness, read as follows: "All of you are children of light and of the day. We belong neither to darkness, nor to night." As I was listening to this—one of the charter documents of my religious tradition—my heart was silently screaming "No!"; for without a doubt, if I am anything at all, it is a child of night darkness. Since my youngest years, and especially since adopting astronomy as a principal interest, I have looked forward with hope and joy to sunsets and oncoming nights, a counter-attitude to a thousand religious metaphors. As I slumped in the pew, I felt for a moment like a spiritual orphan, unable to receive the "good news" like everyone else.

Affinity to darkness and the night is one of several disenfranchisements from biblically based religion that afflict identifiable groupings of individuals, exclusions that range from the relatively harmless to the quite serious. Left-handers have to endure repeated references to a position of preferment at the right hand of the Father and other "rightward" honorifics. More unsettling are the passages that can wound infertile couples, such as Genesis 29, where God seems to manipulate the procreative faculties of Leah and Rachel. Hannah's bargaining with God for a son and even the beloved Magnificat can be painful in this context. And perhaps no one experiences a greater isolation from so much in biblical literature as the human person who happens to be a female.

Scripture scholars and biblical theologians will immediately say that I have missed the point, that by the technique of "hermeneutics" all of these passages should be "retrieved" for their spiritual meaning; properly understood, no one falls outside the canopy of their positive intent. I certainly concur and in my heart believe they are right; it's just that at first contact these scripture passages can sting the excluded party. Indeed, long after that person has understood their esoteric meaning, a fresh hearing can still cause momentary alienation.

And so it is with my love affair with night darkness. Except for a few notable passages—Psalm 19 comes to mind, and even here night gets only equal billing with day—the Bible has cast darkness and the night right behind the devil as the villains of the piece. From "The people who walked in darkness have seen a great light" (Isaiah 9) to "If he goes walking at night, he will stumble" (John 11), the negative metaphor-making goes on, extending to dozens of passages. Revelation 22 describes a scene horrible to contemplate for one with the shape of my soul: "and the night shall be no more." And this is forever! More damaging still, in Luke's account of the arrest in Gethsemani, Jesus describes the turn of events as the "triumph of darkness" (Luke 22:53); and, even worse, as Judas emerges from the Last Supper en route to conspire with the temple guards, John's Gospel adds the powerfully laconic "and it was night." Thus elements that I love—nay, through which I have felt the touch of God—are forever linked with the most odious act of betrayal in history. The "dark side of the force," indeed.

What to do? My answer is simple. As a Catholic, I come from the religion of the great "ands": scripture and tradition; grace and nature; faith and reason. Why not, to paraphrase Cole Porter, day *and* night? I love my religious denomination and faith history; I love night darkness, too. This has been true from almost the beginning of my life, certainly is now, and I pray will ever be. In short, I will ignore the negative comparisons and have it both ways.

My adoration of night darkness is so complete that I measure my spiritual rhythms by the Dark Run. The Dark Run is the name some astronomers and amateur observers give to that portion of the month when the moon is "out of the way," that is, roughly from its last quarter phase to first quarter. During this portion of the moon's monthly cycle, its disk is illuminated half or less, because it is located ninety degrees or less from the sun as seen from an earthbound perspective. Thus, not only is the moon not shining at full candlepower, it is also relatively close to the sun in the sky. The sun, in effect, "lassoes" the moon, like George Bailey wanted to do for his love in *It's a Wonderful Life*, pulling it down quickly after sunset or preventing it from rising too soon before sunrise. A good portion of the night hours are then bathed in deep darkness, the bane of humankind throughout most of its history, but a great balm for some, including me.

The Dark Run is critical to astronomers and amateur enthusiasts, since it is only then that the distant secrets of the universe—galaxies, star clusters, and nebulae—can be seen dimly against the black sky, and its importance in this regard is inversely proportional to the size of a telescope. With my small refractor, only the darkest of skies will give me the chance of viewing the faint lights that call to humankind across the gulf of space. This phenomenon may not be apparent to those who do not regularly scan the heavens. I have seen calendar art and even computer screen savers picturing a fully illuminated lunar disk set against an inky sky. But, in nature, such is not the case. When the moon is full or nearly full, its powerful globe scatters light across the heavens, banishing all but the bright and secondarily bright stars from the firmament; and, in the blackness turned now a more comfortable blue, the Milky Way is put to flight.

Over time I have become something of a Dark Run purist. Now the only moon that satisfies me is an evening crescent of the kind that finds its way into so many of Van Gogh's paintings such as *Starry Night (Cypress with Moon)* or *Road with Cypresses*. Not only is such a lunar apparition beautiful, with pale "earthshine" held so tenuously in its slender arms, but it is shortly to disappear for the night at the behest of Brother Sun. Yet, I know that the succeeding evening, and the one after that, will find it growing in luminescent power and nighttime longevity, ending my brief seasonal romp in the divine darkness.

In saying this, I fear I am committing an act of *lèse majesté* against the consort and consoling surrogate of the Great Sol. The moon at her full powers has been the champion of a humanity terrified for so many centuries by the demons of night; the inspiration for so much poetry; the consummating element for so many lovers; and ever the friend of the mediaeval farmer, hurrying to gather in crops at the autumnal equinox. Who can say a word against her? Only a dolt, immune to the beauty of creation, could fail to be moved by a full moonrise. And even I can admit that the stars and the full moon—at least those that are visible with the moon—make for a lovely tableau. But, in the end, one has to know oneself; and, for

11

me, the journey home is most clearly seen when the night is at its darkest. With copious apologies to the goddess Diana, I confess to being the most un-moonstruck of men.

When the calendar has announced the last quarter moon, I know that the Dark Run has safely arrived, and the festivities can begin. For the next ten days or so, on clear nights, I can repair to the outdoors after twilight to renew my spirit. Often this will be with telescope or mounted binoculars and a previously prepared observing program. Other times, *sans* equipment and discrete observing objectives, the evening will consist solely of drinking in sidereal wonders with the unaided eye.

Out so often under the sky, I have become something of a connoisseur of these limited "seasons of darkness." Of the twelve or thirteen Dark Runs in a year, each offers a slightly different flavor. The Dark Runs occurring from August to late September are alive with the urgent music of insects instinctually aware of the imminent close of the time of warmth and frenetic activity. Later in autumn, the Pleiades grace the east with their presence and remind us of the enduring truth that the greatest of treasures may be of diminutive size. The Dark Run of mid- to late December features the constellation Cygnus the Swan now transformed into the Northern Cross, standing erect on the western horizon in time for the Feast of the Nativity. And all of the Dark Runs of winter are suffused with the blessed, though only relative, silence of humankind confined inside, close to home and hearth, and animal life in hibernation.

But, above all these, the Dark Run of my greatest desire is that of high spring—in religious tradition, the season of

Pentecostal gifts, of the offering of first fruits, of the Buddha's enlightenment; in nature, the brief interval of fully emergent new life, occurring from mid-May to early June and extending slightly in both directions depending on the vagaries of weather. It is then that one can glimpse in the daylight hours what I have come to call the precious "green on blue": the leaves in full foliage against the sky a deep azure, almost as crystalline as in winter, but now in a warmer, more hospitable clime, yet still not warm enough to generate the vaporous air to come in summer. When night falls in the Dark Run after such a day, enchantment is in the air. The night is the blacker due to the obscuring power of new leaves on the trees, allowing me to luxuriate in a bath of darkness, feeling safer and more at peace than at any other time. With a clear sky, the procession of celestial treasures across the heavens can begin: for binoculars, the lovely congestion of stars known as Coma Berenices, said in legend to be the tresses of an ancient Egyptian queen, sacrificed to Aphrodite in thanksgiving for the safe return of her husband from battle; for larger instruments, clusters of galaxies in the region of the constellation Virgo, minute elliptical beacons, shining from unimaginable distances; and for the unaided eye, the Big Dipper, high aloft and upside down, as if tossed heavenward by some impatient god. On such a night, God has only to add a gentle breeze and my joy is complete.

Why is it, I keep asking myself, that something so wonderful to me cannot be deployed metaphorically to describe the Good, the True, and the Beautiful? Why does humankind wish to avoid speaking of darkness, when darkness is such a loyal companion to life's journey? For me, the beginning of an answer is found in the writings of the American theologian

Reinhold Niebuhr, especially in his magistral *The Nature and Destiny of Man*. Man, Niebuhr says, is a problem to himself: he cannot escape his kinship with animals, yet knows himself also to be something more, something different, something ... other. But in the long history of human self-reflection, the inclination, more often than not, has been to avoid living with the tension—to refuse to accept the semi-darkness of the not-fully-revealed "answer" to the human riddle—but to resolve the question one way or the other: either human beings are simply lucky primates and the human drama is "all sound and fury, signifying nothing"; or they are to be understood predominantly as spirits, just passing through this life, while endowed with complete, detailed, and fully functional knowledge of their otherworldly origin and destination. The spirituality of the Dark Run is the beginning of the cure for these unacceptable alternatives, this cleft within the collective soul of humanity.

But first, how to describe in a word or phrase the essential "twoness" of the human condition? One epithet that caught my eye and with which I have stayed is "killer angels," the memorable title of a memorable book about the Civil War battle of Gettysburg. In the screenplay adapted from the book for the movie *Gettysburg*, the term emerges from a conversation between Joshua Lawrence Chamberlain, colonel of the Twentieth Maine Regiment, and his first sergeant "Buster" Kilrain, as they struggle to make sense of humankind in a quiet moment before the siege of Little Round Top—Chamberlain seeing the angelic form and noble matter of the human race; Kilrain, unpersuaded, responding with a litany of the cruelty and degradation that he has witnessed at the hands of man, "the killer."

The phrase "killer angel" is not entirely useful. It does not explain—but then, as a two-word epithet, how could it?—the origin and full nature of evil, an intractable metaphysical reef that has shipwrecked theologians and philosophers for centuries. It also seems to imply that human beings are composed of two discrete—and, therefore, neat—hemispheres. Niebuhr, for one, will have none of this. Says he: mankind is still a creature in the highest spiritual dimensions of his existence and reveals elements of the image of God in the lowliest aspects of his life. Still, when allowance is made for these defects, "killer angels" remains helpful simply because it is vivid and arresting imagery for what I take to be the universal experience of human beings before high-toned thought systems have bludgeoned it into insensibility—namely, their vision of themselves as combination beings, their intuitional perception of living life along a seam, however jagged and indistinct.

In this regard, G. K. Chesterton once playfully wondered whether people who were enthralled with the spiritual side of reality and pointedly critical of earthly life thought that they were "house hunting." As he said, for humankind, this world, this earth, this slough of finiteness elicits loyalty before either admiration or antipathy. We are here; this is our home! That is the stuff of being human. Yet, as Niebuhr says, the human race lives in an environment of eternity, the principle of whose understanding is beyond comprehension, beyond "here." That is human too. Thus, the seam!

Away from this commonsense idea, humanity is ever on the march under the banners of assorted gnosticisms, ideologies, and visionary utopias—systems that pretend to a certainty and finality that is, at least in my view, alien to the human existential situation. But ever and always, there is one place and one time that calls human beings home, if only they will listen—the night sky of the Dark Run. There and then, the stars, like a virtuoso on a keyboard, play on our intuition the sonata of eternity; and yet the music is distant, the theme muted—resonant with the "not yet." The upward gaze is at the same time a bow of the head in a prayer as faint lights speak to us, amid unanswered questions, the word so much resisted—"It is all right! It is your glory to be eternal and yet in time. Embrace the semi-darkness, because it is there that you were meant to see!"

But who or what means us to see in this way? This brings us to the other side of the Great Question: God. It is here too that the spirituality of the Dark Run is such a salutary counterpoise to the major religions of the world, in the domain of one of which I happily find my home.

The great traditional faith-systems, by and large, proceed from Revelation—a climactic or mysterious event by which the transmission of otherwordly knowledge is vouchsafed to a founding avatar or avatars—all of which subsequently repeated or recorded for the benefit of future adherents. Without such sacred knowledge, religions could not proceed, could not continue in being: there would be nothing to talk about, codify, celebrate, re-understand or re-interpret. Revelation, if the expression can be pardoned, is the "mother's milk" of organized religion. But in the realm of religious discourse, the spirituality of the Dark Run stands ready to remind us that, not only is there much of Eternal Truth that we do not know, but there is much that we don't know even about that which we believe we know.

For instance, one of the most precious mysteries given to the human race through religious revelation is the idea/truth that God is a person and, as such, accessible even at the level of intimacy. Emerging in a singular way from Judaism and finding a powerful dogmatic voice in the Christian doctrine of the Incarnation, the belief in a personal God has been a consolation to the millions who have held fast to it down through the centuries. It is also well-known that in much of the religious tradition of the East the emphasis is not so strong in this direction. The Hindu theological edifice, which has dwelling places for literally thousands of gods and divine appearances, nevertheless also insists on the notion of the *Nirguna Brahman*, or God without attributes, of whom *nothing* can be said. In this way of thinking, which finds its inspiration in the *Upanishads*, at one and the same time as one images God, there is a countervailing voice insisting "not so, not so."

Lest one think that the religions of the West, such as Christianity, utterly reject this perspective, the New Testament will provide a curative. In a breathtakingly lovely passage from the Gospel of John, we are told that in Christ we have seen the only begotten of the Father (i.e., God Himself), full of grace and truth. Yet St. Paul reminds us in the letter to the Philippians, that in the process of becoming a man in Christ, the Son of God "emptied" Himself of His divinity. So, yes, we see God; and no we don't. Similarly, while the sacred writer of the first letter of John asserts that whoever abides in love abides in God, he feels nonetheless moved to preface his remarks with the curiously dissonant cautionary note: "No one has ever seen God." And after centuries of religious experience, doctrinal formulations, theological constructs, iconography, and religious art, the writer of the mediaeval spiritual classic *The Cloud of Unknowing* can still respond to the question of how to think about God by saying simply "I do not know." With this minimalist stance, lovers of the Dark Run feel an instant kinship, except that they will take their "unknowing" under a clear sky.

The spirituality of the Dark Run does not abhor dogma or sacred understandings about the nature of God and the human journey; but it insists that they also be seen as departure points into a mystery. What it fears above all things is the calcification and diminishment of the life of faith into a sort of "salvation technology" or "outcomes-based" religion. A local billboard displays a picture of the Bible with the caption: "When all else fails, read the directions." The directions! As if living were like assembling a machine, the scriptures a manual, and God the foreman of the job; and, for every negative experience, He would be available to point to chapter and verse, saying sweetly: "You missed a step."

Purveyors of this kind of theology, alive and well in the vast smorgasbord that is modern TV, have subjected their followers to a fruitless quest for small-scale certainties—physical health, financial solvency, career success, fulfillment in relationships— none of which is assured here below, even for "God's people," so-called. Their appeal, though in a different accent, is eerily reminiscent of the end run around the future promised in the psychic hotline growth industry. Many TV preachers remind their hearers that, as scripture says, "even the hairs of their heads are numbered"—a guarantee that God is concerned about the nuts and bolts of individual lives. Fair enough. But does that mean that we can mortgage God's beneficence to every outward circumstance, that we can see with clarity and in every detail "His will for our lives" as dawn breaks? Religious leaders and believers who think thus need sometimes to be reminded of other scriptures; for instance Jesus, in speaking to Nicodemus, compares the Spirit to the wind, which can be sensed but not pinned down or located with finality. And they would do better to leave off "expecting a miracle" and content themselves with following God's simple mandate to the prophet Micah to "do right, and to love goodness, and to walk humbly with your God," come what may.

The truth is that humankind lives in the semi-darkness and no spiritual technique will solve every mystery or ensnare divinity into a system of metronomic *quid pro quo*s. Does that mean the human race is left bereft in earthly exile with the Dark Run a cyclical and mocking reminder of unanswered questions and unsatisfied longings? No! The Dark Run teaches us the only way to see, and invites us, if we can be persuaded, to attend to the practical consequences of the ultimate unknowability of God.

This begins with an exercise performed by every astronomer known as "dark adaptation," the process of the widening of the pupils of the eyes to gather in as much light as possible in the night. No serious observer begins his/her work until twenty minutes or so of sitting under the night canopy as gradually fainter and fainter stars can be seen. The regimen of dark adaptation can be compared to "patient acceptance," a gift of the Holy Spirit identified by St. Paul, which, if practiced, yields more and more of the veiled truths that are the object of our quest. Our eyes, as it were, teach us not to resist but, by the very way they were made, show us the way to live in the milieu in which God has put us, spiritually as well as physically.

Perhaps a subtler and more revealing aspect of the physiology of the eyes, which astronomers put to good use, is the phenomenon known as "averted vision"—sometimes referred to as "seeing out of the corner of your eye." The rods in the retina of the eye are more sensitive than the cones at its center, which is why one can paradoxically see faint stellar objects more clearly by not looking directly at them. I have experienced this dozens of times when using my telescope to see faint globular clusters—compact star groupings scattered around our galaxy that appear as tiny "cotton balls" in small instruments. Barely visible at times to my direct glance, they often reveal their presence in detail to my averted gaze.

The practice of averted vision is the key to happiness for observing in the Dark Run and for life here below. On Earth, despite everything that has been revealed, we are still invited to catch glimpses of God out of the corners of our spiritual eyes in nature, in art, in persons, in events, in sorrow, and in joy. I often tell my friends that when I go to the movies I always hope I am going to Mass. For Catholics, attending real Mass is regarding directly the primordial mystery as it has been revealed to this faith community, the theological equivalent of looking at the majesty of the sun. But going to movies, and much else in life, also reveals the Divine Presence just at the corner of the eye, like a dim object of the Dark Run. To take just one cinematic example: for me, the divine countenance can be clearly, if fleetingly, glimpsed in the barn-raising scene in *Witness*, accompanied by Maurice Jarre's incomparable score.

Yet we would not be human if we did not desire more than momentary visions even from those things like the Dark Run that, by their very nature, seem only to urge acceptance of mystery and incompleteness. Those who have resolved the human conundrum roughly on the "killer" side of "killer angels" would likely claim that the stars of night disclose nothing except that there is nothing to be disclosed, that they are mute and indifferent witnesses to the triumphs and tragedies of human life—a view that finds resonance in the stories of Jack London, for instance. One can only think of the ironic beauty of the stars on that fateful night in April 1912 when the *Titanic* sank. Can any compassion for humankind be found in the stars for those who meditate on the "convergence of the twain"—ship and iceberg—of which Thomas Hardy so tremblingly wrote? By contrast, those who see human beings as "angels" believe, like the psalmist, that the stars are instantaneously revelatory of the glory of God. Well and good; but it is not enough! It is assurance we seek—not the foolhardy assurances of a "bartering religion," but a confidence still imbued with generous portions of humility, wonderment, and even wholesome skepticism. Do the stars—can the stars—speak a word of such comfort to this earthly Jerusalem as God once commanded Isaiah?

For me, this is where patient attention to the heavens over time and a gentle acceptance of the holy darkness that attends our lives yield the pearl of great price. Though perhaps it cannot be compared to Revelation, from a lifetime sojourn in the darkness I offer the "message" I have received from the stars when the pupils of my intuition were at their widest. The night sky of the Dark Run is the perennial echo of the two most cherished words in all of sacred scripture, in the holy books of every race and nation: "Fear not." C. S. Lewis, the great Christian author, writes in the preface to *The Screwtape Letters* that when angels and other heavenly personages appeared to earthlings, they were always prefacing their message with this two-word formula. He was lamenting the fact that our image of God in the modern age had become so attenuated, and our relationship with Him so comfortable, that fear or awe doesn't even occur. His point was that these passages were worth consulting as a necessary reminder of the true nature of the One before whose glance heaven and earth take flight.

A point well taken. But though I believe Lewis' diagnosis of modern religion has merit, I take an opposite view of the function of these verses. God and his emissaries say "Fear not!" because that is what humanity desperately needs to be reminded of over and over again. Since the world in the foreground is a puzzle, the cosmos in the background must say at least one thing clearly: "Do not be afraid." If the world is, and always must be, in part a dangerous place for humankind, the universe, responding to our never-failing intuition, reveals itself to be a friendly place. That is what Chesterton meant in describing the person of faith as being "pessimistic" about the world while "optimistic" about the universe.

Human life here and now must ever be without short-term guarantees, while What lies behind it, above it, beyond it, and within it is kindly disposed toward us: this is, in my view, the summit of all religious revelation and, for Christians, is perhaps the central meaning of the Christ-event. We cannot say what tomorrow will bring, but we "see" with unerring, dark-adapted spiritual vision the felicitous end of our journey. To this sacred truth, to this "seamfulness" of the human condition, the night sky of the Dark Run is another testament. It invites us, if only we will, to say "Amen."

(III)

AN OBSERVER'S CHAIR

"The lot marked out for me is my delight: welcome indeed the heritage that falls to me."

Psalm 16

A night of observing is about to begin. A mid-July Dark Run has arrived, and I cannot believe my good luck: a strong cold front moved through last night bringing intense thundershowers and washing the languid summer air uncharacteristically bright and clean. At work earlier today during my lunch break, I looked out to see the much-desired "green on blue" almost as good as during high spring a month and a half ago. At the time I thought that if the clear skies were to hold—and the weatherman had assured me that they would—it should be a superior night for observing.

Now I am on my back deck at home at 9:20 PM to make the final decision—to observe or not to observe. I note with delight that the weatherman's opinion has been vindicated—it should be a great night. Time to go inside and retrieve the equipment;

but, before I do, I decide to perform the time-honored "tour of the horizon" as I have done hundreds of times before beginning an observing session. I look over the roof of my house to the southeast and am confronted immediately with that sickly orange-gray glow that is bequeathed to all suburbanites by nearby central cities. Living northwest and in relatively close proximity to downtown Providence, Rhode Island, the light-polluted southeast, except for an occasionally situated bright planet, is lost to any serious observing. I shift my eyes right to due south and another kind of astronomical disaster. My neighbor's oak tree and my maple stand together at attention on either side of a fence to block out the sky to nearly sixty degrees above the horizon. Switching the observing venue to the front of the house liberates a minimal portion of the sky in this direction but at the Pyrrhic cost of streetlight and headlight interference. My southern sky dilemma means that all the rich star fields of the summer Milky Way near the galactic center in the constellation Sagittarius are lost to me and explains why I often drive elsewhere to set up my telescope. But tomorrow is a work day and the long lingering twilight of summer means postponing observing to at least 10:00 PM. So, I will stay here and look elsewhere in the sky. To the right, improvement comes quickly: my maple and a lower stand of trees at the back of another neighbor's lot make an attractive half-window on the western sky, which is relatively darker since it is in the direction of the less populated areas of the state. This favorable circumstance holds as I rotate steadily north of west to the Pole Star and even beyond to the northeast. Only at due east does the wretched orange begin again. Yes, this is about as good as it gets in my locale; definitely a go!

After re-entering the house I emerge on one of several trips to set up my equipment. The first item is the mounting and stand for the telescope; in this case simply a heavy-duty photographer's tripod. I need only two of the release motions that the locking mechanism of the mounting housing accommodates: vertical— what astronomers call "altitude"—and horizontal—what they term "azimuth." On the flat top of the tripod, known as the "pan head," I have attached a further device with knobs, which replicates these two motions but in gradual increments. The idea is to loosen the locks on the main tripod, pitch and yaw the telescope in the general direction desired, secure the locks, and then hone in on the object of the search in slow motion. On top of this slow motion control is attached the circular clamp that will surround the tube of the telescope, the next piece I must get.

My telescope is a refractor, the optical design most people think of when the word "telescope" is mentioned—the kind with a lens at the top and an eyepiece at the bottom for the observer. The smallest models, sometimes called spotting scopes, can be held in the hand or mounted on a rifle. My pride and joy has a three-inch glass, quite small to do "serious work," as the writer of one observing manual has it. Indeed, by the standards of advanced amateurs with their large, almost observatory-class instruments, motorized drives, and near-professional research goals, my setup is quite crude. But then my "serious work" is of a perhaps slightly different kind, and for this, my little refractor serves quite nicely. Having securely clamped the telescope into place, I emerge from the house with several additional necessary items, including a case with several eyepieces that will allow me to view the same object at different magnifications; a folding table; and the so-called "astronomer's flashlight." This indispensable observing aid features a red filter over the bulb, allowing an observer to consult charts in the dark without affecting the night vision that would be lost almost instantly using the conventional white bulb.

Now that all the optical pieces are outside adjusting to ambient temperature, I can go inside again to check my observing program for the night. In order to enhance their enjoyment of observing sessions, many amateur astronomers prepare programs in advance, often containing a mixture of old favorites—objects they have seen many times before—and potential new conquests, my list being no exception to this rule. I check through my clipboard with its several pages of maps redrawn from my star atlas, the printing in which is now too small for me to use comfortably in the muted red light of my flashlight. At various places in the constellation map I have drawn dots with small arrows and identifying numbers for the objects I want to find. At the bottom of the map I have written out in tabular form basic data about the celestial objects, copied out of an observing handbook.

Among the "old" targets of tonight's survey are globular star clusters M-13 and M-92 in the constellation Hercules, and M-10 and M-12 in Ophiuchus, the serpent-bearer. The "M" stands for Messier, after Charles Messier, an eighteenth-century French observer who made a catalogue of such objects. Messier was interested in discovering comets—luminescent snowballs in orbit around the sun—so he made a list of stellar associations that in a small telescope could easily be mistaken for them, even though these associations are deep in galactic or inter-galactic space. There is irony here. Completion of this list of objects—definitely not of M. Messier's affection; indeed, he likely regarded them as a nuisance—has become a standard observing goal of many amateurs. In fact, around March of every year it is possible, due to the favorable placement of the sun, to view the entire catalogue of over one hundred objects in one night (that is, if one is willing to stay up from dusk till dawn)—a phenomenon that has generated a delightful bit of astronomical insanity known as the "Messier Marathon."

I flip a couple of pages and locate some of the new objects I will be searching for tonight. These include a small stellar assemblage or open cluster, technically known as NGC (i.e., New General Catalogue) No. 6633, located in the northeastern sector of the constellation Ophiuchus, and several double stars. The observation of double and multiple stars—distant suns, most of which are rotating around a common center of gravity—has become a distinct pleasure for me. The initial film of the *Star Wars* trilogy has a scene in which Luke Skywalker pensively observes the sunset of the double star system of his home planet—a nifty and imaginative bit of movie making— though the chances of life on a planet in such a system may be slim. In spite of the fact that the components of double stars are millions of miles apart, the systems themselves are at distances of multiple light years from earth and, as a result, the stars will appear as one unless magnified by a telescope. Telescopes of varying sizes have corresponding limits—measured in degrees, minutes, and seconds of an arc—down to which they will be able to "split" or "resolve" the components of a double. It is always fun to test the limit of your telescope, but the choices I have made for tonight I know by experience will be comfortably within my scope's range. They are all in the constellation Cepheus, The King, and are designated Struve 2816, 2819, and 2840—after Wilhelm Struve, who made a catalogue of hundreds of double stars based on observations made from Dorpat Observatory in what is now Estonia in the years 1824–1827. As I bring the observing program out I quickly check to see if Cepheus, a circumpolar constellation that comes into prominence in early to mid-summer, is high enough in the northeast to observe or if I will begin my program with the other objects. As I put my observing list on the table, I see that the irregular quadrilateral of Cepheus, with its apex star pointed toward the Pole, is nearly high enough to allow for observation now.

It is time now to get the last piece of equipment I will need for tonight's session—the chair! My observing chair, that is. I could have brought it up on one of the other trips, but I usually make a ritual of leaving it until last, to be carried alone. This is altogether right and fitting for a sacred object extracted from the tabernacle of my family's history. I used to leave it in the farthest reaches of my cellar, so that I would have the sense of entering the holy of holies when retrieving it. But since this area is the location of the furnace, I have since thought better of it and now store it with the rest of my astronomical gear. It is unprepossessing in appearance—a simple folding chair with a green plaid fabric, like thousands used at the beach or in parks. Being an older model, its seat has only two large pieces of crossed fabric, unlike the more conventional "slats" common today; and as such, it has held up remarkably well in its over fifty years of use, with only slight fraying in some sections.

Unfolding it out on the deck, I smile at the anticipated pleasure of sitting in it for a few minutes while my eyes finish their adaptation to the night. Simple tactile contact with this holy artifact is uniquely bracing to my spirit; gently passing my hand over the arm supports is like rubbing a crystal ball with results, however, in the inverse—I see ever more clearly, but it is the past. Coming into view from the gauze of memory is my grandmother, smiling beneficently at me while sitting in the chair the first time I remember seeing it as a post-toddler of four or five. It was on a roofless, third-floor porch of our cold-water flat on another July night so long ago. For "the night before the Fourth" we were all assembled to see the fireworks to be displayed from the local municipal stadium: "we" being my mother, father, sister, brother, grandmother, grandfather, tenants from the lower floors who didn't have a good view, an aunt, uncle, and cousin from up the street—the company changed from year to year; but, that being my first time, it just seemed crowded to me.

A fidgety and impatient kid up well past his bedtime, I had been making the rounds of every adult on the porch, asking the same question: "When do the fireworks start?" and receiving the same answer: "When it's dark!"—sometimes accompanied by an indulgent pat on the head and later, after the patience of my hearers waned due to multiple inquiries, curt dismissals. Except from my grandmother. She was all forbearance as she repeated the unsatisfying mantra. When it's dark! How could I be expected to know that July third, coming a mere two weeks after the summer solstice, was one of the longer days of the year? I only knew or, better, sensed, as I looked west where the sun had recently set, that dusk was deepening with agonizing slowness.

I heard my grandfather say "Here comes Mr. Kelly." As one, we shifted our eyes downward to see a tall man with thinning hair dressed in khaki, striding confidently down the street. It was reliably rumored that Mr. Kelly owned a car, but most people, it seemed, had never actually seen him drive it. He preferred to walk, and on previous excursions had passed me by with a smile when I was playing on the sidewalk under the watchful eye of my sister or cousin. To this day, it is Mr. Kelly that I see in my imagination whenever I read Ray Bradbury's chilling science fiction short story "The Pedestrian." When he got within range he waved to the assemblage on the porch, but my father and grandfather had already begun talking in low tones, knowingly, as men will sometimes do, if they feel they have the inside scoop.

I strained to hear what they were saying, but caught only threads of the conversation. The term "fire department" went speeding by. Mr. Kelly, it appeared, was a firefighter, one of the few professions that was already familiar to me. After filing that datum away, I went back to listening: " … has to go to the stadium to supervise.…" I had no idea what "supervise" meant, but intuited from my father's tone and Mr. Kelly's age that he might be an important fireman. While I was struggling with the implications of that, my grandfather announced matter-of-factly: "Yeah, they're probably waiting for him." Whether that was actually true or not I prefer to leave as lost in the mist of legend; I only know that my grandfather's words had hardly exited his mouth, when an incandescent bulb came alight in my mind with an interior report like that of a nineteenth-century camera. It was Mr. Kelly, someone I actually knew, who was the answer to all my pyrotechnic yearnings and those of hundreds of other kids around the city. The fireworks would start when *he* got to the stadium! My eyes widened to saucers as my jaw went slack: the Father Christmas of Fourth of July eve was passing by. Mr. Kelly turned the corner of our street and disappeared, and I immediately began a series of desperate mental calculations concerning how long it would take him to get to the stadium; but I had no idea how far it was and no developed time/distance sense as yet. I gave it up with the vain hope that Mr. Kelly had broken into a jog.

I looked west once more and then at the faces of my relatives in animated conversation. I dare not ask them again, my fledgling common sense told me. Yet I had to do something to force the onset of the fireworks. I had two shreds of evidence about what might bring the outcome devoutly to be wished: Mr. Kelly and darkness. About Mr. Kelly, I could do nothing. Could I hurry darkness? I had to try. From somewhere within the recesses of a brain grasping at the few inferential straws available to a four- or five-year old, an unshakeable truth emerged: when it is dark, the stars are out. I smiled at the simplicity of this bit of information probably conveyed to me by my mother since, going to bed on or before the coming of darkness on most nights, I had had few occasions for adequate verification. No matter, it was all I had; I would test the veracity of her contention tonight.

I picked a spot somewhere (it seemed to me) near the middle of the porch but actually, as it turned out, dangerously close to the banister. I stared straight up and resolved not to move until I had located a star. Little did I realize then how many hundreds of times in the future I would in similar fashion look longingly to the heavens of the oncoming night. Nor did I realize how the balance of my life would turn the experience on end; for I would not hereafter be looking to the stars for signals of the mundane, such as fireworks, but for their own fair beauty and, in due time, I would embark on the quest for one in particular: a mysterious and inviting star at the end of a wondrous river.

It was a clear night, but seconds passed, and still I had not located any stars. I started to feel a little uncomfortable; and then, slightly dizzy, I began to sway. Suddenly, from out of nowhere it seemed, a huge hand grasped me by the forearm. "Stop that!" It was my father's command from the other end of a wristlock. Evidently I had careened too close to the shaky railing and was in imminent danger of falling thirty-five feet to the pavement. The thunder of Mount Sinai was in my father's voice and the everlasting fire of the burning bush in his eyes. The intensity of his anger astonished me, almost brought tears. In retrospect, I realize how on edge he must have been with such a jittery kid making his maiden voyage on a porch that would likely not meet minimum housing standards for safety today. He quickly followed up: "What do you think you're doing?" The indignation was still there but dialed back about 75 percent. "I was looking for a star," I stammered.

Stars! The very word took on life as I spoke it in the midst of the hushed company watching my reprimand. They began looking to the heavens too and speaking to the issue. My grandmother wondered where to look to see the Big Dipper; my grandfather told of the darkness of skies and brightness of stars in the countryside where he was brought up; my sister mentioned the astronomy book she received as a gift the Christmas before. I looked from face to face with wonderment as the conversational transaction moved as fast as a basketball on a fast break; and my momentary sorrow turned to joy: I had actually started a conversation, my first experience of being socially useful.

My father pointed due south to where the fireworks were supposed to appear and said, "There! That's probably Mars!" We all looked in that direction and saw a red jewel twinkling low in the sky. A very good guess, but it probably was the star Antares, often mistaken for the angry red planet. Now the race was on in earnest, as everyone began to say "There's one!" or "Over here!" All the bright stars of summer were quickly captured: stars with names now familiar to me—Vega, Altair, Deneb, Arcturus—some brighter than Antares; stars that I could have seen a few minutes before when I first looked up, except that I was trying too hard to see them and looking in only one place. Then began the search for the secondarily bright stars or, hopefully, the Milky Way; and, as this holy game continued, I began to entertain a heresy—maybe the fireworks could wait!

Presently my mother emerged from the kitchen with fruit—cherries, plums, watermelon—and we all took a break from the enterprise and subsided into a period of quiet munching. When it was drawing to a close my anxiety began to rise again about the fireworks—or, would the stars, now manifestly out, be enough? The thought was aborted as the first projectile was suddenly sent heavenward from the stadium. In my imagination, Mr. Kelly, standing on a raised platform in the middle of the field, had just dropped his arm as if he were starting the Indy 500 or the chariot race in *Ben-Hur*. For the moment at least, the siren song of the fireworks banished all thought of stars from my mind. At the conclusion of the display, I was immediately lead away by my mother to a long-overdue appointment with bedtime, my grandmother giving me a final benediction as I left the porch. After my mother withdrew from my bedroom, I found it hard to sleep. The night was electric with activity: firecrackers exploding, people laughing and talking in neighboring yards. When my consciousness did begin to falter, my last thoughts were surprisingly not of fireworks, but of my grandmother sitting in her chair—and of stars.

The next day was the continuance of the family feast of Independence Day and took the form of a larger gathering in one of two places—the country house of Aunt Lucy or of Aunt Kate—sisters of my grandmother. Aunt Kate had married a farmer—my kindly Uncle Walter—who must have had one of the last local full-process dairy farms: he owned a herd of cows, milked them with the help of family members and hired hands, pasteurized the milk, and delivered it to customers in his own trucks. His farm was like a new world to me. I remember wandering off after dinner with my cousins to listen to the hum of the purifying machines, watch the grazing of the cows, stare wide-eyed at the enormous bull, and look in wonderment at my uncle's rolltop desk, in front of which he would now and then sit at the close of the holiday and talk to us with what seemed genuine interest.

More often the gathering was held at my Aunt Lucy's. She was the youngest of my grandmother's sisters and, having married late in life, was the occupant of the ancestral homestead. The property was somewhat more remote than my Uncle Walter's and was improved with a relatively simple cottage once lived in by my great-grandfather and that, in my earliest years, had no indoor plumbing. When arriving at this family shrine on the Fourth of July, my grandmother always carried her folded chair herself, for some reason not wanting to surrender it to anyone else to tote. We urban-dwelling kids, once the car doors were opened, were overtaken by a temporary and tonic frenzy much like being let out of a cage. Of course we played games—hide and go seek, badminton, softball—but the greater pleasure was to be had in exploring woods and fields of a kind we were not accustomed to in our own neighborhoods. The grown-ups sat and talked, played cards under the trees, or pitched horseshoes. Dinner featured sweet corn harvested on-site by Uncle Karl, Aunt Lucy's husband; the usual hot dogs and hamburgers with condiments; and—after all, this was southern New England—clam chowder.

A staple after-dinner activity was the walk to the family cemetery plot. On one such occasion, my cousin Alice alerted me for the first time to take care not to walk on the graves "out of respect for the dead"—beginning in me a strain of sensibility about those who have been gathered into eternity that is with me to the present day. The most prominent headstone was that of my great-grandfather—Charles Pierce, 1851–1923—descendent of Michael Pierce, who came to this country in the 1640s and was killed in a skirmish in 1676 during King Philip's War. A stone monument commemorating the incident stands in deep center of a baseball field near the Blackstone River in Central Falls, Rhode

Island—a delightful nexus for me of two joys, family history and the national pastime. Michael Pierce was himself the progeny of the Pierces and Percys of England, who could trace their family origin from before the Norman Conquest, and who, it appears, now and then played prominent or supporting roles in that country's history.

Below my great-grandfather's name was that of Ida Pierce, 1856–1928—my beloved great-grandmother. An inveterate poetess of simple verse, in 1910 she printed a collection entitled *Home Poems*. Leafing through its pages, one finds celebrations of the joys of country life, of nature, relationships, and religion, and also a chronicle of family triumphs and tragedies: Charles and Ida were the parents of seven daughters who grew to middle and old age and two sons who died as boys.

After sunset, we would pile into the car for the journey home. Often my mother would put me into sleeping attire before departure to ensure expeditious transference into bed at our disembarkation point. A good thing too; for I often dozed on the way back or fell dead asleep. Sometimes I would awaken, and for a minute or so watch my father intensely scanning the road ahead, and then withdraw again into confident sleep.

I know less about my father and his family than I do about the Pierces. Alexander Vincent was the son of Dionis Vincent, son of Ambrose Vincent of Trois Rivieres, Quebec. I remember once at a Vincent family gathering my Aunt Salvina was speaking at length about how the Vincents, despite their modest current situation, were actually related to either the former king of France, to Cardinal Richelieu, or to some other

Gallic luminary. At the end of her interminable disquisition, I saw my father wink to a few listeners and then proceed to ask, "Okay, Salvina, where's all the money?" Howls of laughter from this the sardonic and wholly justified remark of a husband and father who uncomplainingly labored in a textile mill for twenty-seven years before dying an untimely death of cancer.

My mind goes into fast-forward, stopping at twenty years later. My father, grandmother, and grandfather are all dead. My mother is already hobbled by early-onset arthritis, but she is undismayed; for she is about to get a ride in my first car—a Volkswagen Beetle—for an all-day excursion to Plymouth, Massachusetts. It was then that I noticed she had inherited the chair, as I struggled to get it into the less-than-adequate trunk, finally opting for the more suitable backseat. After our arrival, I staked out a spot for her under a convenient shade tree, where she could read her newspaper and book in the now-storied chair, or engage in another favorite activity: people watching. Meanwhile, I took in the sights: the Rock, *Mayflower II*, Plimouth Plantation, and other museums. Every so often I would check back with my mother; but before doing so I would glance from afar as she sat in the chair—I, flitting from attraction to attraction, and she at peace amidst the memorabilia of her own ancestors.

And now, my mother having departed, the chair has come down to me. I smile in gratitude that I have been judged worthy to be a link in the chain of its apostolic succession, even as I struggle to return to the present moment from my reveries. There is a whole night's observing ahead.…

Later, I am back sitting in the chair after having brought all my equipment inside where it is neatly arranged on my desk but not yet packed away—this to insure that condensation on the optical surfaces evaporates before I cover them. The evening's observing is over, and a triumphant tour it was. Struve 2840 was a gorgeous double star, the components featuring, at least to my eyes, a green/yellow color contrast. Better yet, due to a misreading of my astronomical handbook, I was rewarded with a delightful surprise: Struve 2816 is actually a triple star! My mind transfers easily from these conquests to incidents in family history as I linger outside for a while.

Scanning the heavens in my solitude, I find myself glancing around at intervals to the rear of the chair. There in my mind's eye I see gathered my parents, grandparents, uncles, and aunts, smiling in assent at my evening's activities; and beyond them, in the temporal distance, faces indistinct, but somehow recognizable, since their blood runs in my veins. I notice also the forms of others not of my family who have departed: teachers, clergy, family friends, next door neighbors who gave me Halloween treats —mentors and well-wishers who spoke a kind word as I journeyed past in my youth. All of these, in their separate ways, have carried me to where I am now, under the starry canopy. Somehow I am doing this observing for them; on behalf of my ancestors and other loved ones, I am the current, and local, duty officer of the Dark Run.

A verse of scripture from the Psalms comes to mind: "The lot You have marked out for me is my delight!" The place to which You have brought me, the person I have become, behold, it is very good! And in no small part it is because of the heritage of family and human association interwoven into the circumstances of my life—positive and yes, even negative—but all of it precious, precisely because it is a gift to me. Sometimes, I feel like the father in the story of the prodigal son, so great is my desire to run out to these who have gone before and encircle them in my thanksgiving.

I look quickly around again and there are the heavens, awaiting my reverential gaze. Yet, if we as human beings are meant to be "pitched out," as Joseph Campbell might say, into the celestial abyss, we must nevertheless come *from* somewhere. I look behind the chair and once more regard the marvelous amplitude and extent of my "fromness." Backward, forward, my glances and my sensibilities alternate, and in between, in the middle—I, in the chair. It is the seam once more!— the commodious knife-edge on which all human life must find balance. My observer's chair is a metaphysical still point between things past and things to come, between the human and the divine, between time and eternity.

The optical surfaces of my equipment are no doubt dry by now; but I will not go in just yet. I cannot tear myself away; for here reposed in the chair, as much as any human being can be, I am sitting ... home.

(IV)

THE ECSTASY OF SOMEWHERE

"There's a place for us ... somewhere."

(*West Side Story*)

Dorothy in *The Wizard of Oz* found joy in traveling to "somewhere" beyond the rainbow and in returning home, one more literary testament to the spiritual power of places. It was places and my childhood reaction to them that constituted my first set of mystical experiences, in which Dorothy had a role as well. I say "set" because, although they were separate, they were somehow as one; indeed, the recognition that they were one was what made them mystical.

It began in that third-floor flat that I remember as my first home. The interior architecture was curiously structured, with my sister's bedroom perhaps the chief oddity. It was a simple rectangular space, entered at the long end, but with a sudden narrow alcove jutting right at the other. The alcove had the main window for the room, and therein lay its fatal flaw; for the space, too small for any other use, begged for storage. At various times bureaus, dressers, and/or piles of boxes were jammed into the small area, partially or significantly blocking out the light and ventilation of the window. The space, as real-estate appraisers would describe it, had inherently contradictory and therefore low functional utility.

It didn't matter to me. Whenever I was alone in the room, and especially if this was after sunset and my mother had not caught up with me for bedtime, I would jam myself between the current obstruction and the window and gaze out. This facade of the house looked almost due northeast, which consequently became (and has remained) my favorite compass point—northeast, the direction from which most stars seem to emerge in north temperate latitudes. So strong is my affinity for this vector that I sometimes describe my quest for joy as the effort to reach the "utter northeast," rather like the journey to the farthest east of Reepicheep, the kindly mouse in C.S. Lewis' *Chronicles of Narnia*. Needless to say, Cathy and I have traveled on many vacations to Maine and other northeasterly points, and Greenland is never far from my mind. But there was more. Directly athwart the northeast line of sight was the pale green light in the tower of the Industrial National Bank building, tallest edifice in downtown Providence. Mesmerized, my only thought was to get there somehow. Why, I did not know.

Now, the focus shifts to an overcast day when my mother retrieved me from whatever I was doing and said, "We're going to look for your sister." We walked slowly up the hill that was our street, my hand unquestioningly in hers. Up meant west, and because of the remembrance of this experience, it always does so in my mind. (Indeed, later when Cathy and I moved to a new neighborhood, and I noticed a street very similar to that of my childhood, I was momentarily disoriented since it rose in uncanny fashion to the east!) At the top of the hill we paused to survey what lay ahead. Before us rose a steep ridge, much more daunting than the hill we had already climbed. Encumbered by undevelopable topography and full of wild growth, its primary purpose appeared to be to provide a playground for local kids, who cultivated it with their imaginations and referred to it simply as "the woods." My mother and I peered in. On the side of the hill were a series of randomly located boulders, glacial erratics left from the Ice Age, while the slope was everywhere strewn with the leaf detritus of a hundred autumns past—a woodland seemingly "dark and deep," like so many Cathy and I have subsequently hiked in the holy ground that is New England.

Suddenly our recess was over and in we plunged. We took a slanting path up, my mother obviously not enjoying the more rigorous climb, while by now I had come to regard this as a great outing—an unexpected adventure in the dull life of a preschooler. The path was for the most part clear, but here and there we had to clamber over fallen trees and, in some areas of loose soil, secure our footing. I had a couple of sliding "accidents," which did not improve my mother's disposition. Finally, we wound around a large tree as the path doubled back toward the lip of the hill, from which extended a large green field. Off to the side was another huge tree, but this one had a u-shaped double trunk. Ensconced on either side of the "u" were my sister Barbara and my cousin Jan, deep in intimate conversation and passing a box of crackers back and forth. What were they talking about? Careers, marriage, what they were going to do tomorrow? I do not know; but so help me, the scene struck me with such unexplainable joy that I was momentarily afraid. It was somehow utter beatitude—as in John Hicks' painting *The Peaceable Kingdom*, but for the moment with no animals in sight.

My mother and I advanced over to them for a conference. I cannot remember if she delivered a remonstrance or was just telling them to come home because the family was going somewhere. As the monologue became a colloquy, I was left unattended for the barest of intervals. In that moment, I stared out across the green field and saw a distant row of trees and houses—"nothing special", as it were; though I have traveled there by bicycle many times subsequently to try to recapture the experience. As I continued to stare, I remember that I swallowed hard, a most unusual thing for a young boy to do, unless he were discovered with his hand illegitimately in the cookie jar. What was I looking at that would make me do such a thing? Or was it that Something was looking at me? In any case, in an instant the spell was broken, and we were all heading home.

The third and last episode in this mystical triptych occurred somewhat later when my sister Barbara told me she was taking me to the movies—to *The Wizard of Oz* in one of its last theatrical releases before its long-running serial exposure on TV. For some reason I at first refused to go, unthinkingly attached to whatever I was doing, and thereby nearly missing out on a minor theophany. My sister patiently but determinedly overcame my resistance, and we were soon on a bus to downtown Providence. Once inside the theater and with the first strains of the credits score, I was captured and have been a *Wizard of Oz* evangelist ever since.

Over the years I have spun my Oz theories and interpretations to anyone who would listen and to decidedly mixed reviews. I love reflecting on how the story has a universal resonance because it is about a journey home or about how the companions of Dorothy are really aspects of her soul—intellect (Scarecrow), emotions (Tin Man), and will (Lion). When I was reading about Hinduism in my college career, I was struck by how closely the companions of Dorothy reflected the various "yogas" or pathways to God—the way to God through knowledge (Jnana Yoga—Scarecrow); the way to God through love (Bhaktic Yoga—Tin Man); and the way to God through work/action (Karma Yoga—Lion). Finally, I fully embraced the wonderful, barely veiled message that the companions during the journey began to love Dorothy more than they wanted the gifts they were seeking, and in the process of trying to save her, discovered they already possessed the ingenuity, the affection, and the bravery that were their goals. In this aspect, *The Wizard of Oz* teaches the maxim variously stated by sages down through history, of which Matthew 6:33 is an especially good version: "Seek ye first the Kingdom of God and its righteousness, and all these things will be added unto you."

All this lay in the future as my sister and I watched the movie that day. I was all agog as every episode in the story unfolded; but at one point something happened, the tectonic plates of my soul shifted, and I had seen something with my inner eye. By the end of the movie, I had not figured it out, so there was only one thing to do—desperate situations call for desperate measures—I begged my sister to see the movie again. I can still remember Barbara calling from a phone booth outside the theater after the second showing, trying to allay our mother's fears and having great success because for once, having unaccountably lost track of time, she had not yet expected us.

I cannot be sure even now that the repeated viewing revealed the answer to my conscious mind that day; but it assuredly imprinted itself on my subconscious, because I feel now I have a sense of what it was. For this most precious experience within an experience, for this revelation, I owe immeasurable gratitude to an oft-overlooked but crucial contributor to the joy of cinema: the art director; in this case, the team of Cedric Gibbons and William Horning. For in the scene where the four companions emerged from the woodland and first beheld the Emerald City, I was given perhaps the closest thing in mystical perpendicularity to one who is most often an ascender of the inclined plane. I did not see this scene; I recognized it. I had seen it before, in the pale green light of the Industrial National Bank Tower and in the emergence from the woods with my mother on to the great green field. As my imagination again takes hold of these memories, I can almost envision the events, sequential in experience, slowly rising up to a height and forming a pathway out of time into a divine precinct. After this, proofs of the existence of God, while fun to entertain and discuss, were for me supererogatory.

What I had found was the mystical presence, the numinous "place" within me. But it was actuated in my case by the physical experience of places: enclosures, expanses, enclosures as seen from expanses, and expanses as seen from enclosures. I have come to call this divine signature on my soul "the ecstasy of somewhere" or, to pass grammatical muster, "the ecstasy of being somewhere." As I have matured into manhood, the irresistibility of this personal tendency has begun more and more to overtake me. And it is not just the usual locales— meadows, woodlands, mountains, seashore—that have this mysterious power; now the oddest places and crevices can pull on my spirit so tenaciously that I have to turn around and take note of them.

For instance, interior stairways. In their retirement, my mother and my aunt lived in the same apartment building, and I would often visit them both on a given day. Bypassing the elevator, I would take the seldom-used stairway—the building was a complex in which mostly elderly people lived—to transit between apartments. As soon as I closed the fire door and began the ascent or descent, a remarkable sense of well-being would come over me. What was it and why now? It was, I truly believe, the Hidden Being of stairways awaiting the rare pilgrim through its premises to take note of its presence—as surely as the cave paintings at Lascaux were held in purposeful abeyance for centuries until the first explorer beheld their magnificence.

Another venue which has for me an irradiating power—and this an unusual one for a devotee of the Dark Run—are the well-lit aisles of supermarkets, perhaps at some time other than the hours of peak business. To me, this place has always seemed like a universe within a universe—with rows upon rows of well-stocked shelves awaiting the countless decisions of customers to enter them into a personally crafted order reflecting individual tastes and the respective exigencies of life. Watching chance meetings of people who talk over temporarily immobile shopping carts with seemingly no thought for finishing their chores and utterly at peace, I have sniffed the aroma of eternity, where *being* has the final victory over *doing.*

Having found traces of Divinity in such unlikely places as stairways and supermarkets, I have begun to look for it everywhere. Sometimes in odd or transitional moments within rooms, I find myself looking into corners where walls and ceilings meet. What does the universe look like from there—this perspective point created by humankind under the inspiration of God? It was in analyzing this singular desire to know, to experience more of completeness, as it were, that was the beginning of my understanding of the other side of the seam—the inescapable seam—cohabiting with the ecstasy of being somewhere.

I came to a fuller realization of this on one of our family vacations to the near reaches of the utter northeast—Maine—when we crossed the forty-fifth parallel of latitude at the town of Perry. The Chamber of Commerce or some other civic booster organization had proudly displayed the municipality's claim to fame on the welcome sign, bringing Cathy and me to a screeching halt for a photograph. I stood on what I hoped was the exact spot and peered north and then south, overcome with the idea that I was exactly halfway from the equator to the Pole. I pivoted to east and west and suddenly was shot through with a sense of poverty of spirit as I wondered about all the souls who live along this line in Europe and deep into Russia or the other way across the United States. I recognized it as akin to a feeling I have often had about Route 44—a secondary connector road that begins (or ends) at the Atlantic Ocean near Plymouth, Massachusetts, extends westward across southeastern Massachusetts, continues through Rhode Island, passing near my home, and disappears over the western horizon into Connecticut and beyond. What if all the people who live or work along this artery, I sometimes muse, could somehow be brought together? For what? I have no answer to this question; my longing for such a gathering seems to me somehow sufficient.

The name I have given this impulse, this sense of the privation of being, is "the ache of particularity." It is really the mirror image of the ecstasy of being somewhere, since it is essentially the sorrow that one cannot be *everywhere* and with *everyone*. It is the longing that the human soul can at times be heir to when looking at or into the lives of others with whom it is not connected by ties of blood or friendship. Watching the random itineraries of shoppers in the suburban malls, I have found myself wishing that I could somehow be a part of their lives. During trips on expressways, as I view the exit ramps speeding past and note the signs directing travelers to unfamiliar places—squares, minor streets, villages, and suburban localities—I have this unexplainable urge to tear them down and take them with me, so great is my appetite to know about them; but more, to understand what they mean in all their affective power to those who call them home. To plumb so wide a depth is likely the prerogative of God alone; yet in one of the preparatory prayers preceding the consecration at Mass it is said that Christ humbled himself to take on our humanity that he might, through such a process, give us a share in divine life. Whenever the priest utters these words, I find myself praying for *this* morsel of Divinity—to taste the meaning of places, all places, as they have lived in the affections of my brothers and sisters of the Earth.

The momentum of all these sentiments—aches and ecstasies—has grown so large in my consciousness that it has veered into the region of the other coordinating axis of existence: time. Now I am a devotee of the "ecstasy of sometime" as well. One can find this joy in various ways, most notably in art, another name for which could be "time celebration." Music, for example, exists only in time and gives its blessings then and then alone. And the visual arts such as painting are often an attempt to capture the rapture of moments. The work of Monet is an excellent testament to this phenomenon, especially his repeated paintings of the same object—grain stacks, memorably—to record the ever-changing play of light.

My personal way into this ecstasy takes several additional forms, a notable one involving the "liturgical year" of my favorite spectator sport: baseball. Though its inner nature—the conduct of its play, the game itself—is conducted marvelously and, in contradistinction to so many other sports, without regard to time limits, its outward dynamic, its pilgrimage as it were, moves with the times and the seasons of life. There is spring baseball, when, the slate wiped clean from debacles past, hopefulness is in the air for teams in every league from T-ball to the majors, including my beloved Boston Red Sox. The crack of the bat barely escapes the fall of the last snows, as kites fill the sky and hormones drive animals from their lairs to indulge appetites held too long in check. Summer finds baseball's essence mostly perfectly merged with its concurrent existences in a thousand stadia from sea to shining sea. The still air—whether dry or humid—is the milieu of choice to view a classically executed hit-and-run or to abide the little eternity wherein the pitcher gets the sign before delivering the ball. Then, and finally, there is autumnal baseball and the consummation of the playoffs and the World Series. Thank God, the simultaneity of the match-ups in the Division Series and the League Championship Series forces the baseball owners to allow a number of day games. It is in these final days that the uniforms seem the most beautiful, set off as they are by the encroaching shadows of October, while the determined men inside them participate in epic dramas of three to seven acts. Seen in its entirety, baseball is for me a joy; but savored in its time-envalued parts, ecstasy.

Then there are Civil War encampments and battle re-enactments. It is easy to dismiss this activity and the ardor and perfectionism of its many enthusiasts as an attempt to escape into the past. And yet who can deny that Ken Burns in his PBS series *The Civil War* uncapped a collective American gusher of sentiment and emotion, as many Americans, perhaps heretofore indifferent to the historical ordeal of the North-South struggle, found themselves involuntarily caught up in the mystic chords of memory. What they were experiencing was the ecstasy of *that* time—the soul's assent to a temporal passage that, despite the horrible carnage, seems for a variety of reasons somehow peculiarly pregnant with the divine presence; and, because humankind inhabits eternity as well, the ecstasies of *that* time are forever accessible. At its most poignant, the ecstasy of *that* time is the exploration of one's own past in which event-landscapes are sometimes so transformed and elevated that they seem to comprise a kind of personal beatific vision.

If ecstasy can be found in the past, it surely can be experienced in components of time that are cyclical and returning. Friends are sometimes astonished when I relate that Ash Wednesday is one of my favorite days of the year. This seemingly innocuous mid-week day, raised to a peculiar dignity, inaugurates the Christian equivalent of "March Madness" i.e., Lent—a season of enhanced striving, peppered with abstentions major and minor, all ordered to capture the April prize of everlasting life. Watching Christians, myself included, streaming en masse to churches in the attractive grayness of low spring (i.e., late winter) to receive the outward sign of hoped-for repentance and growth, I am somehow elated. I love to meet people in the fish and chips store later, who, noticing that I am similarly marked, nod or smile in restrained recognition. No other process or activity speaks to me so strongly of the collective journey of the human family; or, as one insightful priest once sermonized, there is no greater meaning to Ash Wednesday than the communication of the truth that we are in this—this struggle, this life, this victory—together.

Though I cherish these opportunities, the search for time-ecstasy must always, in the end, bring me back to the night sky. For many years now I have kept a log of my astronomical observations. Two logs, actually. One is chronological, the other ordered by constellation. After entering a night's observations in the first log, I later transfer them to the second—the idea being that, having recorded what in a particular constellation

I have seen, I will not re-view it but look for something new. It doesn't always work out that way, however; my inclination is to return to old favorites again and again.

My chronological log is a relatively simple affair. There is a notation about starting time, locality of observing session (usually my backyard), and the "seeing" and sky transparency, followed by a list of the objects I have seen by catalogue number and description. Looking over past sessions, I see remarks such as "the star cluster was best at 48 power"; or, "I was able to split the double star at 60 power but not less, and the fainter companion seemed to have a golden hue"; or even a one-word exclamation, "magnificent." In essence, the log is simply a recording of the form, "I saw X on this particular night"; but it all depends on how one says it. In the screenplay of *A Man for All Seasons*, Robert Bolt has Sir Thomas More say to the Duke of Norfolk in defense of his conviction that Henry VIII cannot by fiat make himself head of the Church: "I believe it…. No, no, it's that *I* believe it." Likewise, I not only *saw*, but *I* saw; and, in that ecstasy-moment, I recapitulated in my own being the habit of God who, as the author of Genesis 1 tells us, looked over and over again at the things he had just made.

So much of the literature and hymnology recalling God the Creator is utterly adulatory of Him, who was the Spinner of galaxies and Fomenter of the Big Bang—the evangelical Protestant (and now Catholic) devotional song "How Great Thou Art" being a noteworthy example. The faith dynamic implied here is a movement from beholding the beauty of the created to an immediate ascription of praise and honor to the One who made it.

Nothing illegitimate here, perhaps; but a close reading of the first chapter of Genesis may suggest a different spiritual trajectory. It is hard to escape the notion that there is something of a self-forgetfulness in God's activity, caught up as He is not in the fact that *He* is making something, but that He is making *something*. In other words, while God's behavior is, as I have claimed, like mine, it is in another sense its reciprocal; for just as it is crucial to recall that it is *I* who look, and am thus raised to the dignity of observer, it is essential that God, for the moment, not stand on His dignity as Creator, that he may descend to the station of my fellow-observer. And, joined together, we gaze at the spiraling galaxies and behold, they are very good!

"God saw how good it was!" is in fact the formula used to describe His repeated creational disposition in one of the translations of the first chapter of Genesis. The phrase is echoed in another later incident in the Christian scriptures where Peter, accompanying Jesus and two other disciples up the mount of Transfiguration, beholds Christ's glory together with that of Elijah and Moses and blurts out, "How good it is for us to be here!" Unfortunately, he quickly follows up with the inapposite suggestion: "Let us build three booths, one for you, one for Elijah, and one for Moses." To which offering, he is immediately corrected from a Voice out of a cloud, identifying the unique status of Jesus.

Poor Peter! So often the fall guy of the Gospel narratives, constantly taking one step forward and two back, taking a stab at things when the other disciples are silent (sometimes literally, as in John 18:10) and, more often than not, taking it on the chin ("Get thee behind me, Satan!"). So here on the mount of Transfiguration he makes a classic blunder in order that the sacred author may clarify for all future readers the singularity of Jesus in the universe and in salvation history. Lost in the theological shuffle is Peter's initial intuition, equally as compelling for all humankind, of how desirable it is, how satisfying to every longing, simply to be in God's presence. In creation, in transfiguration, in life, and yes, in death, God sings and man responds: "How good it is, how good it is to be here, how good it is to be ... here ... now!"

"Be Here Now!" A simple three-word prayer formula, it emerged in the 1960s and was made popular by Baba Ram Dass, Alan Watts, and others, eventually becoming the last line of a memorable song by James Taylor entitled simply "New Hymn." I confess I love the phrase—it seems to be a genuine spiritual ejaculation flowing from all those who have experienced space-time ecstasy. The truest syllables of every existential yearning, the Lord's Prayer of all religions—the words convey at once a reflexive injunction and a divine invocation. Along the frontier adjoining those two intentionalities lies the domain of all human felicity.

For the spaces—domestic and cosmic—that have delighted and moved me; for the times that have enlarged my being; for the endless possibilities of subdividable joy to be found where points, lines, and planes intersect moments, seasons, and years, I give thanks to You, O God, and implore You, everywhere and always, "Be Here Now!"

(V)

THE PRAYER OF GOOSEFLESH

"All flesh is grass." Isaiah 40:6

"In my flesh shall I see God." Job 19:26

What are we to say of the human body, vilified in so much ancient philosophy and lionized in scores of infomercials for exercise equipment and health club memberships? Ambivalence indeed appears to be the most characteristic human attitude when all the thoughts and doings on the subject throughout history are averaged out. The Bible, and the Christian faith in particular, is no exception to this rule. "The spirit is willing, but the flesh is weak," says Jesus—an overarching judgment, borne out by history, and supported elsewhere in the sacred text with copious lists of the sins to which the flesh is heir. One is just about to slough off this mortal coil, philosophically at least, when one is brought up short by St. Paul's claim that the body is the temple of the Holy Spirit and by the creed's insistence on the resurrection of the body—of all things!

Students of the biblical etymologies of "body" and "flesh" will note, perhaps disapprovingly, that I have conflated the two concepts. It is true that they are most often sharply distinguished in scripture—"body" being typically seen as an object of transformation, "flesh" of corruption. Yet it is also true that the two terms are sometimes used interchangeably and that it is "flesh" that in a few noteworthy cases ("and the Word became flesh") is chosen for the higher calling.

Academic quibbles aside, I find the on-balance positive thrust of my religious tradition in this area to be a bracing tonic when, after jogging or working out on the cross-country skiing machine, I end up gazing at my body/flesh in the mirror with manifest displeasure. This ... thing ... that I wish I could change or trade in for, is somehow important, very important. Indeed, when one is reminded that the Greek and Latin words for "breath" and "breathing" are closely related to that of "spirit," it becomes clear that God's presence in the body is finely enmeshed, tempting one to say (playing a bit fast and loose with an exegesis of Job 19:26) that "In my own flesh I see God"—a notion that would have appalled Plato.

If God—God the Holy Spirit in the Christian symbolization—is conceived of as comfortably and happily ensconced in the nooks and crannies of our bodies, it makes more poignant the biblical injunction to "do nothing to sadden the Holy Spirit." Seen in this context, despising one's body diminishes the universe in an act of unthinking sacrilege. Jesus also warned his followers to avoid blaspheming against the Holy Ghost—an offense more deadly than abuse hurled at Himself. This sin, the only one said to be unforgivable, has tantalized scholars down through the centuries. What could it be that it is accounted by God as more serious (at least in the eternal disposition of things) than rape, murder, treason, or hatred of His own Son?

Is self-hatred the answer—the self, which the Spirit blesses as home, the individuated existence for which the body is the necessary condition and only sensible expression? It may be that for this kind of hatred, persisted in and insisted upon, there is indeed no cure, even for God. And this blasphemy is sometimes larger and therefore more sinister than the singular case, a malignancy that has many faces, many names. One is racism, which among other things is a collective body-hatred acquiesced to by a victimized group after centuries of coercion. It is painful but necessary to imagine persons fingering their own skin or feeling the contours of their noses and eyes and wishing in near despair that somehow it were not so, that they looked like someone else. This truly is blasphemy, but the blasphemer is not the one who harbors these sentiments; rather it is the regime, the social structure, the moral (immoral) atmosphere, the heritage that has brought the victims to such a place. God deliver us from ever participating in any process the end result of which is to make others despise what they see when they look in the mirror.

There are thorny philosophical dilemmas to resolve and serious moral issues to confront when thinking about the human body; that much is clear. For guidance in beginning a thought-journey such as this, I am inclined to consult a mentor or authority of one kind or another. For me, more often than not, it is Clive Staples Lewis, a name that has already appeared more than once in these pages. Lewis, the celebrated Oxford don and literary historian, has become something of a publishing phenomenon, almost an industry, since his death in 1963. Outside the domain of his technical specialty—mediaeval and Renaissance literature—where he did some groundbreaking studies, he found time to write a raft of books dealing with his avocations of religion and theology from varying perspectives: science fiction, children's stories, apologetics, fantasy, and autobiography. After a high school friend loaned me a copy of *The Screwtape Letters* I was immediately captivated, and devoured as much Lewis as I could throughout my college career, attracted above all to his gift for imaging the invisible things for which we all yearn. I see Lewis not so much as an all-encompassing guru but as a modest guide, genial conversation partner, well-wisher, and spiritual godfather—St. Clive, always there to invoke when the matter at hand relates to the eternal verities. At my most hopeful, I see my own thinking as a reflection and extension of his: personal variations on most desirable themes.

And so it was that I came to treasure a little-remarked-upon Lewis essay—originally a Pentecost sermon—entitled "Transposition." The scriptural story for the day was the descent of the Holy Spirit on the original apostolic community, producing all sorts of weird bodily phenomena—prophesying, speaking in foreign tongues—as the Spirit seized the initially terrified followers of Jesus. From this, Lewis brought his listeners into a consideration of the relationship between the physical and the spiritual in human life. He argued that the spiritual realm, being a richer domain, was forced to express itself bodily using responses that had to cover other functions as well. The classic example is tears, which can be triggered by allergies or dust particles in the eye, but also flow from anguish or joy. Lewis compared this to acute angles in a painting which may have to do double duty because of the two-dimensional nature of this form of representational art. Sometimes painted acute angles are just that—say, a picture of a slightly opened pair of scissors—and sometimes they stand for right angles—say, the corner of a building—due to the exigencies of perspective. Likewise, the body is in one sense just what it is and in another stands for and expresses invisible realities to which it is linked, making do with whatever physical processes it can command or, better, allow to be commanded. Lewis sees these concepts as the beginning point—to be worked out later by scholarly professionals—in a philosophy of the Christian sacraments.

In my own case, they were the stimulus for a more deliberate pattern of observing the body and what I have come to call the body's "envelope"—the body seen in its dynamic mode as it is animated by the human soul. I have already mentioned tears. Virgil, in treating of life's difficulties and sorrows, had coined the term *lacrimae rerum*, literally "the tears of things"; but reality—that is, "things"—if rightly engaged, also brings one to tears of joy, gladness at the simple fact of being. As traditional philosophy saw it, "knowing" was a process of entertaining a series of related concepts that captured and formally contained the "real," thereby yielding understanding and, at a further remove, technological applications. Tears are the result of a kind of knowing, too—the recognition that we try to express in the declaration "I know it in my bones." There is a suggestion here that the body "knows" something of which the mind, preoccupied with the manipulation and ordering of concepts, is ignorant. The reflexive nature of tears as an expression of such knowledge hints at promptings far deeper in the mystery of the human person than mental operations. It is as if something or Someone cannot wait for the mind to draw the inference and express the related conclusion, for instance, "Yes, this is beautiful"; so the body is pressed into service.

I have observed this in another bodily function: breathing. Of course, the relationship of this phenomenon to things spiritual is nothing new and hardly needs to be remarked upon. In the religions of the East, breath control, practiced under certain kinds of yoga, is integral to the achievement of psychic transport to a state of bliss. My experience is more modest but still awe-striking. I once had a friend, a music teacher, who, when I remarked that one of my favorite pieces of music was the *Fantasia on a Theme by Thomas Tallis* by Vaughn Williams, responded with a long, slow exhale while staring intently into the middle distance. The effect was startling; it appeared to me that the Holy Ghost had emptied out of his body, swirled about the room, and embraced us both in an eddy of mutual assent, an inverse Pentecost of silence. The wordlessness lasted for long seconds; and when the conversation did resume, it was about music in general with only oblique references to the Williams piece. Neither of us wished to fracture or diminish a unity of apperception by direct comment; for it was clear that our experience of the beauty of the *Fantasia* was as one; his very life's breath had told me so.

And now to what I lovingly refer to as "my stigmata"— gooseflesh—mine and that of countless millions, since the human experience of these skin bumps is well-nigh universal. Here is a situation that conveniently fits the Lewisian theory:

goose bumps can make their appearance due to cold weather or, alternatively, to reasons having nothing to do with temperature; for instance at certain sublime moments such as birth, life passages, and death. In the latter cases, the tripwire often seems to be appropriate music added to such solemn occasions, but sometimes music alone can do it. I have a mental register of compositions that produce this response in me even after, or perhaps especially because of, repeated hearings. One such is the Second Symphony of Brahms, a piece I treasure all the more since it, unlike many others on the list, is able to generate goose bumps on my body when I merely listen to it in my mind! In addition to music and depending on the mysterious workings of my disposition, I can get gooseflesh from the hearing of certain words, the entertaining of ideas, and of course from the vision of the night sky.

The locales on my body of this goose skin are also a source of wonder to me. The primary locus is my head, which experiences a pressure at the temples and a circle of feeling around the cheeks and neck. The other prominently affected region, somewhat surprisingly, is the calves, which seem surrounded by a cylinder of intense energy in moments of rapture, reaching the thighs in certain exceptional cases. I had begun to notice myself longing for the gooseflesh instead of simply acquiescing in its onset, a disposition that brought me to a remarkable conclusion one night while I was writing monthly bills at my desk and listening to music. As the compact disc player gave forth the short piece "Walk to the Bunkhouse" from Aaron Copland's orchestral suite *The Red Pony*, I watched the gooseflesh slowly form—this time on my forearms—and made a simple internal declaration: "My body is at prayer!"

And why not? If tears are a form of knowledge and breath communication, why cannot goose bumps be accounted intimacy with the divine? What conclusion can one come to, other than that the body sometimes turns Jesus' insight on its head—the spirit is indeed willing, but sometimes, with the aid of goose bumps, the flesh beats it at its own game. The body is certainly a less refined medium for divine activity than the soul, as Lewis says, but what it lacks in suppleness it makes up for in immediacy of response, running ahead of the soul at times to achieve oneness with the source of truth and beauty.

But our flesh is much more than even this. Seen in its dynamic aspect, as shepherded by the soul (But what would shepherds be without sheep?), it generates a perceptible aura or penumbra, which in its sum total makes up what I like to call the "blessed individuation." The "individ'l," for whom the scarecrow in *The Wizard of Oz* would untangle every riddle, is endowed with a holy separateness implicit in God's very breathing out of creation—a "shooting star" trajectory that He fully intended to be enjoyed, at least for now and in some ways forever, for its dazzling distinctiveness. I am not speaking here of the false individualism of the current age: an amalgam of ubiquitous tattoos, fashion statements, and crude bumper-sticker maxims. These are counterfeits precisely because they have not taken stock of the quiet, modest manifestations of individuation that are available to us all, ironically ceding such expressions to unappointed tastemakers, self-styled trendsetters, or even manufacturers responding to test-marketing and focus groups.

The joy of genuine singularity can be found rather in such overlooked human faculties as, for instance, penmanship.

The thrill of looking at old letters is partly contained in the perception that the ideas and emotions expressed on the page are being conveyed in the person's own hand. At another level, one sees penmanship married to a written task such as shopping lists. I look with delight at the shorthand creation that Cathy uses to facilitate her market forays—with the days of the week neatly inscribed across the top and sections for produce, canned goods, and paper goods strategically placed on the page for convenient check-off as the mission proceeds. Wallets and pocketbooks, arrangements of dresser drawers and closets are also instances of the body's trail of individuality, not to mention signature laughter, facial expressions, habits, tics, and hobbies. Within the walls of homes on holidays, families indulge in reminiscence, often of those gathered into eternity, with sincere and sometimes backhanded encomia to just such uniquenesses.

Cathy has always been the stronger of the two of us on the critical importance of the body-individual. Confronted with notions of an eternity characterized by absorption into some kind of undifferentiated oneness—the residuum of conversations where I have been at my oversimplifying worst—she has instinctively rebelled, holding fast to Job's breathtaking declaration that it will be he himself—not some other being—who will behold the divine epiphany in the everlasting habitations. Others are not persuaded; though it is not the prospect of being dissolved into some everlasting beatific soup that fills them with dread, but the more chilling thought of extinction, pure and simple. In a somber poem John Updike asks a direct question: "Who will do this again?"—"this" being the life's journey of an individual analogized as a thrilling theater performance, savored by others precisely for its poignant irreplaceability. The answer is given in the poem's dark title—"Perfection Wasted"—a two-word fusillade at death's refusal to be quenched even when faced with the high tapestry of a human life.

If such perfection is to be vindicated rather than wasted, it may be that the body holds the key to an understanding of how; for the flesh, the medium through which the sacred individualism is experienced is also the curative for the terror of isolation that individualism threatens. I am speaking of sex—one of the means that the body provides to the self to escape self without annihilating self. In my faith, the voyage of sexuality is shared with a lifetime companion in a covenant unto death. But I have no intention here of making the case for the sanctity of matrimony or the importance of marriage in the larger social order—that is work for others, and God's blessing on them; I only offer what I have experienced.

I start with a term with a Catholic resonance—*communicatio in sacris*—literally, the "sharing in holy things." It is applied to the sacrament of the Eucharist —the ritual by which the Body and Blood of Christ is "confected" (i.e., made present) and the mechanism (a meal) by which sacred—nay, divine—reality is distributed and received. Students of doctrine are ever in the process of refining the theological paradigm—"changed substances under perduring appearances," or "spiritually transfinalized matter"—that explains how all this takes place, certainly a legitimate and much-smiled-upon exercise, but one which must take its proper place in the sequential flow of sacramental life. At the beginning there is a claim. The thing (wafer) that the communicant holds in his or her hand or receives on the tongue has become something other, higher, and deeper; and the first human response brackets off all paradigms and even creeds: one must eat. Once again, the body—as in tears, breath, and gooseflesh—takes a decidedly, if temporary, leadership role. And so it is with sex. Lovers have always known instinctively, if not explicitly, that sexual relations are festooned with doorways and passages to the depth of life and meaning—the immemorial poetry and, until relatively recently, the music of love gave univocal testimony to it. Sages and moralists throughout the ages have been right to teach that sex severed from such bonds and connections is ultimately destructive of humanity. Still, the journey through the door begins with the body; and in the process, custody of the body no longer resides exclusively with the individual; it is consecrated precisely because it now also belongs to someone else. *Communicatio in sacris.*

The larger implications of this process bring to mind a story related by Viktor Frankl, the theorist of human psychology and concentration camp survivor. His passing in September 1997 was overshadowed by the contemporaneous deaths of Princess Diana and Mother Teresa; but his legacy, contained in such works intended for a lay audience as *Man's Search for Meaning*, may prove as resilient. In a particularly moving passage from that wonderful book, he tells of how the image of his wife sustained him in the utter desolation of Auschwitz, as he carried on imaginary conversations with her and savored her smile and countenance. Though she was already dead, it counted for nothing; what they had become together was stronger than death and helped Frankl, more than anything else, to understand the triumph of love and divine beauty.

I have never been in an existential situation as extreme, but thoughts of my own wife seemed to loom as large in an experience I had a few years ago. While I was graduate student in Boston, Cathy and I lived for several years in a small apartment —one side of a kind of duplex—in Newton, Massachusetts. We subsequently moved back to Rhode Island; and when it came close to the time to take comprehensive exams, I made a number of trips alone up Route 95 for days in the library. After one long session, as I was heading home, the thought entered my head to drive by our old place. Stopping the car across the street from the apartment where we had spent the first few years of our marriage, I gazed at the house for what seemed an eternity. We had once dwelled here, where we learned to love each other, sat on the porch, received visitors, put up Christmas trees, walked the surrounding streets. Little seemed different in the scene, yet it was totally changed, changed because of the simple fact that we once occupied this space—our collective consciousness was a part of the history of the neighborhood. Like the prow of a ship, our lives had cut into this little portion of the ocean of space-time, rearranging it astern forever; our time together in this place mattered in a way not fully comprehensible here below. Overwhelmed by the heady theological implications of all this, sensed rather than in any measure known, I lay my head on the steering wheel and closed my eyes. It was then that I realized that all this time, just below the level of consciousness, held at bay while I entertained lofty thoughts, but now no longer containable, was this incident's greatest truth: I missed Cathy's presence bodily.

Such thoughts and experiences have convinced me that the body in some way is linked with the mystery of eternal life—a not-too-breathtaking conclusion for a communicant of the Christian faith that, despite temptations to the contrary in its early history, has continued to teach the resurrection of the body as well as of the soul. The Resurrection narratives in the Gospel of John are a balm to Cathy and many others as they see Jesus, though able to pass effortlessly through walls, also being recognized bodily by the disciples. He is even seen cooking a meal! Happily it seems there may be something to my intimations about tears, breath, and gooseflesh.

But not sex! The body, that most perishable of things, has paradoxically been the most persuasive in teaching us to yearn for immortality; then there is a religion that, unlike many others, accords the body a place at the table in eternity; and yet that same religious tradition denies to the glorified body the fleshly function that is most in tune with the divine music.

Or so it seems. I am thinking here of an incident in the life of Jesus where He appears to pronounce definitively on the matter—a confrontational debate with the Sadducees—recorded with minor variations in the Synoptic Gospels (Matthew, Mark, and Luke). The Sadducees, the religious party of the priestly aristocracy, were guardians of the Torah, the collection of writings with ultimate primacy in the Revelation to the Jewish people. Of innovations in Judaism since the time of the final editing of the Torah, the Sadducees would have none. One such was belief in a personal resurrection, a notion favored by Jesus. To reduce this new-fangled heresy to the absurdity they believed it was, they disingenuously posed to Jesus a casuistical dilemma straight out of the book of Deuteronomy, one ordinance of which dictated that if a man died having no children, his brother was to marry the widow to raise up progeny to the deceased, whose name would therefore not be blotted out of Israel. The Sadducees related a tale of seven brothers who, to fulfill this imperative, married the same woman in succession after the death of each. Whose wife would she be, they wanted to know, at the Resurrection?

Reading the text, one can almost feel Jesus' frustration with the use of what amounts to a techno-legal conundrum to wound and destroy a sacred, if inchoate, human hope not yet fully codified in the Judaic patrimony. To seize the main point, He put a rhetorical sword thrust through the distracting side-issue of the seven nuptials—"When people rise from the dead, they neither marry nor are given in marriage"—and then, alluding to broad hints in the Torah, made an earnest appeal to his interlocutors to affirm that God is a God of the living not the dead, that is, to believe in the Resurrection. Meanwhile, those married persons standing at the periphery in witness of this remarkable scene—and, yes, we *are* standing at the periphery, not just reading the Bible; for these stories of sacred scripture are living events in which to some degree we participate!—seek to console themselves as they see the precious co-created artifact of their married life canceled out in a flash and deemed unfit for eternity. Eyeing each other, with whom they will have no married bond in the region of the everlasting bliss, they are reduced to bittersweet bromides: "Ah well, at least we'll live forever; we'll have victory over death; we'll be like angels, as Jesus says; it will be wonderful!"

It will not do. However eloquent our rationalizations, however ingenious our mental gamesmanship, our bodies—the doorway through which we passed into the depths of love—will not be quiet; frantically heralding that (in the repellent phrase of common currency) "there is something wrong with this picture." My body, my friend whom I have come to trust, cannot be lightly dismissed in this matter; and yet it seems to be objecting to forthright declarations coming from the highest authority. Is there any way out of this dilemma?

One ray of hope remains, but it requires a shameless reading into the text of this story. I do so without hesitation, led on as I believe I am by unerring intuition. At the outset, I call to my aid and defense an unlikely ally—unlikely because he was so much more interested in the mind than the body—the nineteenth-century German idealist philosopher Georg Wilhelm Friedrich Hegel. Most college introductory philosophy courses touch lightly on Hegel; to go any deeper requires entry into the impenetrable thicket of his technical language, described by one commentator as nearly incomprehensible. Yet one tenet of his vast system, compelling in its simplicity, attracted interest from the very beginning. I am speaking of the dialectical method, by which Hegel described the continuing journey of the human mind in an onward and upward spiral. Reduced to its lowest terms, this interpretive principle stipulated that every idea (thesis) in due course generated its opposite (antithesis) and, in the ideational clash, a new concept was born that somehow reconciled them by rising above the plane of their contention (synthesis).

It was inevitable that Hegel's paradigm, with its neat threefold structure and recognizable analogues in so much of human experience, would be instantly pillaged even by those thinkers who rejected just about everything else in the great German's output. One such was Karl Marx, who, in another case of turning an idea on its head, applied the dialectic not to the evolutionary workings of the human spirit but to the seemingly never-ending historical class struggle, that, appearing in various opposing theses—slave/master, serf/lord, proletariat/capitalist—would eventually result in the synthesis of socialism. An earlier miner of the Hegelian mother lode—F.C. Baur—deployed the dialectic in the field of biblical interpretation—specifically, the study of Christian origins. For churchmen and scholars through the centuries, the New Testament record was in places rather unsettling, revealing clashes between Peter and Paul, legalism vs. libertarianism, and various other sectarian struggles—all desperately needing to be explained, especially in a text deemed to be inerrant. For Baur, however, this dilemma was merely proper grist for the Hegelian mill. The conflicting Pauline and Petrine stances, for instance, recorded at some length in the book of Acts and alluded to in the Epistles were, you see, simply the thesis and antithesis of the formative Christian idea, of which the emerging Church of several centuries later, with its settled creeds, canons, and liturgy, was the glorious synthesis.

The thing is irresistible, and therein lies its danger. Like Communist spies to a McCarthyite, to a fully immersed Hegelian the dialectic is everywhere. Reality cannot speak except in triads, and therefore—at least this is the view of some critics of Hegel—it is more Hegel than reality that we discover. They will get no argument from me. I hold no brief for the universal applicability of Hegel's system; it is the innards of the idea of the dialectic that I am chiefly interested in and what I believe veil a universal truth. This can be found in the German verb forms that Hegel used to describe the process dynamics of the dialectic: *aufheben*, which contains within it the idea of "to cancel" and yet somehow "to preserve," and *aufgehoben*, which essentially equates to "transcended without being fully discarded." The English word most closely approximating this concept is "sublation" ("cancellation in the process of elevation")—three syllables to which I now cling for dear life or, better, wear like a religious medal.

One element remains to be inserted before I apply my grand design to the issue at hand: support for the contention that Jesus did not reveal everything of substance in his earthly ministry. In a pithy and, in the manner of popular proverbs of the day, embarrassingly direct exhortation to his disciples, Jesus urged them to refrain from "casting their pearls before swine"—"swine" being those who were actively hostile to the Gospel message. The Sadducees, at least in this incident, certainly qualified. Had it been otherwise; had they been sincere in their desire to understand, he might have revealed something more of the deep mystery that surrounds the redemption of the human race. But "swine" could also be those who, for quite understandable reasons, were simply unprepared for the paradoxes and further refinements of the truths of the Kingdom. Among this group were the disciples themselves, whom Jesus frankly told at the Last Supper: "I have much more to tell you, but you cannot bear it now." He promised the Holy Spirit would in due course guide them "into all truth."

I now invoke that Spirit's blessing on what I am to write—a quasi-Hegelian gloss on Jesus versus the Sadducees. Simply stated, it is this: in earthly life people are routinely married and are given in marriage (thesis); in the heavenly kingdom, in the life beyond death, on Jesus' authority, they do not and are not married (antithesis)—but that is because marriage, as well as all that is good and touched with the divine signature in human life, will be raised to a new synthesis. This was the secret that the Sadducees, because of the hardness of their hearts, could not hear; this is one of the mysterious references of the words "salvation" and "redemption" that, from one perspective, are really terms for "sublation" dressed up in theological garb.

Those mystics who have spoken to the issue in the long history of human curiosity about the afterlife have at one and the same time told of its joy and beauty and counseled against trying too strongly to visualize or otherwise imagine "what it is like." But if eternal bliss is more—so much more—than terrestrial life, it cannot be less; different, it cannot be sheerly different. That is the gift to us of the doctrine of the resurrection of the body.

Cathy and I nurse a fantasy about a possible life together beyond death. She loves trees; I love stars. Whoever passes on first will wait for the other; and then, reunited, we will live for a thousand years within trees, proceeding on to the stars for a millennium or more, returning to the trees or wherever else our fancy takes us. Behind me I sense the pitying glances of those who no doubt see this as a desperate attempt to hold onto this life: both materialists, affirming that nothing exists except matter in motion and that human lives, any human lives, will dissipate into the elements from which they came; but also traditional believers, counseling against trying to shape heaven along the contours of our own desires. As for Cathy and me, we understand that the image we have created, with its visual and time-bound constraints, is at best a metaphor, one born of love. But what are metaphors but the yoking of seemingly unlike entities—flouting reason and common sense—at the behest of something, call it "poetic imagination," call it the Holy Spirit, that impels us in this direction? The moon is clearly not "a ghostly galleon tossed upon cloudy seas"; yet our souls say to this kind of seeing: "Yes, a thousand times, yes."

If the body can be saved, if individuation can be redeemed, if Job can say of the vision of God, "I, myself, shall see," why cannot all that Love has given birth to, made larger and wider, also endure? Cathy and I have an answer to this question: somehow it will be also we *together* who will see. Faith it is that sustains our assent to such a bright prospect, but our first teachers in this school of wisdom were our own bodies.

(VI)

THE ROAD TO FROSTY DREW

"Now we see through a glass darkly."

(I Corinthians 13)

It's something of a family joke how much, it is claimed, I enjoy the postponement of gratification—the root of this "maladjustment" being attributed to a Puritan heritage that I have embraced and most others of my tribe have more or less spurned. As might be expected, I don't quite see it that way or, rather, choose to describe the symptomatology in different (my relatives might say spin-doctored) terms. To me, postponement is simply another name for anticipation, in which somehow fulfillment already lives. My mentor, C.S. Lewis, describes a permutation of this experience when, living with his tutor during his late boyhood, he would tramp the countryside of Surrey and find himself already savoring the joys he would experience in his reading that night.

A similar interplay is seen in the correlatives "journey" and "destination" and is best summed up in the colloquialism "getting there is half the fun." In the theological symbolizations of Christianity, the "destination" is the Kingdom of God, ushered in at the End Time with tribulations, but also with the justice and vindication for which the suffering faithful yearn; and yet Jesus is at pains to remind his loyal followers that the Kingdom of God is also "here" and "now," "within [their] midst." The history of journey literature is replete with such ambivalences. On the road to Oz, the companions already sense a presence with them and within them, yet they are impelled onward to find the wizard, who essentially confirms their inner transformations. Similarly, on the road to Emmaus, the resurrected Jesus is at all times with the disciples, a truth they grasp dimly, finally recognizing Him only upon arrival in the village. It must always and ever be for the things of the spirit—we must journey to an end but are called to discover the end in the journey.

Such a quest, such a road looms large in my life—the road to Frosty Drew. Though I have made many pilgrimages there already—fewer now than in years past—it is a terminus to which I am always journeying in anticipatory joy of the next time. Frosty Drew? Begin with Edwin F. "Frosty" Drew, 1948–1976, whose life, like a fireball meteor, was brilliant but brief. After graduation from Brown University, he began a career as a writer and found himself drawn to use his gifts to raise public awareness about the preservation of a disappearing natural heritage, especially in his native southern Rhode Island. After his untimely death, the public, whose attention he had finally focused, endowed a nature center and wildlife refuge in the town of Charlestown, within the territorial limits of which is an astronomical observatory that bears his name.

Most of the great observatories of North America are located in the west, southwest, mountainous regions, or dry climates—all of which support the high ratio of clear nights and steady seeing required for intensive research. Coastal New England doesn't qualify on any of these counts; hence Rhode Island has only a handful of small observatories—most associated with colleges or amateur astronomical associations—and only one, Frosty Drew, located at a far enough distance from the metropolitan area to be significantly immune from neon glare and thus enabled to invite into its precincts at nightfall that rarest of commodities, the truly dark sky.

In his *The Civilization of the Renaissance in Italy*, Jacob Burckhardt mentions in passing that large segments of the populace of that era were familiar with the times of the rising and setting of constellations, a corpus of knowledge since rendered superfluous by the advent of clocks. But even if, out of antiquarian interest, one wanted today to re-acquire the skill—rather like taking up the illumination of manuscripts—one would be confronted with an obstacle that never haunted Pico della Mirandola or DaVinci: significant, night-destroying, urban and suburban light pollution. To meet this ever-widening challenge to the night sky, astronomers and other interested parties founded a few years ago an advocacy group—The International Dark Sky Association—which works with lighting engineers, community planners, and government officials to design night lighting responsive to the needs of commerce and security and, at the same time, as protective as possible of astronomical darkness.

Amid the multifarious social ills that afflict us—hunger, poverty, unjust discrimination—protection of the canopy of night darkness will strike some as a low priority indeed. Yet, as is the case with endangered species, we cannot calculate the loss to humanity, to all that humanizes us and elevates our spirits, of the splendor of the heavens. One experience from many sojourns at Frosty Drew was decisive for me in this matter. It was a Dark Run in mid-June: my brother-in-law and I made an impromptu run to Frosty Drew despite some reservations. The night was forecast to be clear before midnight, but incoming fog was expected later along the south coast near Charlestown. As it was the time of the summer solstice, we had to wait until fairly late to begin observing. Forty-five minutes into a pleasant round of objects, my brother-in-law called my attention to the south and east. "Here comes the fog," he lamented. But it wasn't fog; it was the Milky Way—at the horizon! The Milky Way—our galactic center, seen most prominently in the summer sky from the Northern Cross to Sagittarius—is nowadays barely glimpsed when at the zenith; to see it at such a low point in its celestial trajectory where the atmosphere is thickest is rare indeed. I watched as a fog bank of stars, as it were, seemed to advance and engulf us—a vision that has continued to haunt my dreams. No human being should be deprived of such a sight; yet light pollution now threatens to extirpate it from the memory of man.

To deal with my own Milky Way deprivation—forced, as I am, to do most of my observing in the light-blanched skies of suburbia—I must repair periodically to Frosty Drew. Fortunately, the observatory is open every clear Friday night throughout the year. The difference between the observing situations—my backyard versus Frosty Drew—is the difference between attending church and going on retreat. In the days before a projected excursion, my anticipatory juices are running full, my soul suffused with the bliss of pilgrimage. One thing only can bring me back to earth—adverse weather. No such ill fortune crossed my path in the days immediately before a trip to Frosty Drew a few years ago. It was the Dark Run of late October, and my delight was augmented by the fact that a number of other pilgrims dear to me would also be making the trip—the last of the season for many of them, before the late fall and winter cold called a halt to their dark sky enthusiasms. Cathy—no lover of near- or below-freezing temperatures—was one of those who gladly left cold weather observing to me; but she smilingly joined me now in a light supper before packing our equipment in the car for the hour-plus journey to the local cynosure of all things astronomical. This time, instead of my telescope, I decided to take my large 70mm binoculars, a tripod (the binoculars are too heavy to hold for long), a small footstool for child viewers and, of course, the observer's chair.

We swung onto Route 95 for the southward journey from our home in the north of Rhode Island, and then veered off due south as 95 made the more direct vector to the Connecticut shoreline and points southwest. As we approached Charlestown, we were traveling old U.S. Route 1; my last thought before making a left for the wildlife refuge was surprisingly of Key West. I knew what it was. Hanging around in my semi-consciousness was a television documentary broadcast in 1960 or thereabouts in celebration of Route 1, about to be superseded by the Route 95 expressway system as the principal north-south vehicular conduit on the eastern seaboard. Hosted by movie actor Van Heflin, the film featured an auto journey through every state traversed by the now semi-retired route. I vividly remember

Heflin at the beginning of the show standing at the bridge at the Canadian border in Fort Kent, Maine—the "headwaters" of Route 1—and at the end walking its last few feet on a dock in Key West. Route 1 so conceived is another of my "unitary fantasy/aspirations"—as in, "what if everybody living or working along Route 1 could somehow get together?" Before completing the turn I nodded toward Key West in thankful prayer for this personalized symbol of the human yearning for greater and higher unity.

We proceeded down a secondary road to the gates of Ninigret National Wildlife Refuge. By now the darkness of the heavens was overwhelming as the last street light disappeared from view. Entering the gates to the park, we made a couple of turns and were soon on the access road to the observatory— an abnormally wide thoroughfare. My cousin Norm once explained, in response to my query on this, that the road was undoubtedly an aircraft taxiway during World War II, when the ground on which we were now traveling was Charlestown Naval Air Station, a training base for carrier pilots. As we continued, off in the distance we glimpsed the dim red lights that signaled the observatory compound and the barely visible silver dome—a most mysterious enclosure set in an expanse, another Emerald City, in my musings. Still at a reasonable distance, I lowered my illumination to the dimmer lights out of respect for those already observing. We reduced speed and finally inched into the small parking area. We were home!

Well, maybe not ... *home.* As glad as Dorothy and her companions were to see Emerald City, it was not home for them. But here the look of a domicile was well-marked: a white picket fence surrounded a neatly trimmed lawn with a front gate and walkway to the observatory's front door. One half-expected to see a mailbox. Rather than the Emerald City, the "home" that is Frosty Drew is like the Last Homely House East of the Sea in Tolkien's *The Fellowship of the Ring*, where "merely to be there was a cure for weariness, fear, and sadness." Yet that home, like this one, existed primarily as a departure point for an unavoidable journey to transcendence.

Cathy and I began to offload the equipment and entered the rear of the observatory grounds by another gate. I was elated because some of my companions and fellow observers had already arrived with their telescopes: Jerry, a friend from church, and my sister Barbara and cousin Jan and their two husbands—my astronomy buddies—"the two Norms." Cousin-in-law Norm is a man full of lore; a navy veteran and career serviceman, he tells exciting tales of participating in one of the last Bastille Day parades in French Morocco or doing low-flight ice reconnaissance in Alaska. Norm, with his prodigious memory and life experience, is for me something of a living link to history: he used to give weather briefings to Admiral John Buckley who, in his earlier career, had sailed Douglas MacArthur to safety after the fall of the Philippines; better yet, Norm's great-grandfather, whom he knew as a boy, fought at Gettysburg! Besides astronomy, we share an interest in armchair polar exploration.

Then there is brother-in-law Norm—the "abyss jumper." In the family we call the inclination to waive small talk in favor of immediate engagement with the fundamental issues of life and death, the eternal structures of being, or the Great Journey as "jumping into the abyss." Norm is always the first one in. On occasion, I have gone to his house for a scheduled visit and have found him waiting for me on the porch, his finger thrust into a book marking a passage from Carl Jung or Joseph Campbell that he wants to begin discussing even before I take off my coat. I have never met a man so utterly uncaring for the things this world seems to value, or so single-minded in his quest for insights into the mystery of mysteries.

There were hugs all around as Cathy and I greeted everyone and I admired the small telescopes of Jerry and the Norms, already set up and in operation. I went back to retrieve the rest of my equipment while Cath continued to talk. Having opened the chair so that we could all—but especially Jan, Barbara, and I—by turns establish tactile contact with our ancestral history, I attached my binoculars to the top of the tripod by means of a device known as an L-clamp, and in no time was ready to go. My night vision was fairly well adapted by now, but there was one more thing I wanted to do before beginning the observing program. Cathy and I left my binoculars in the care of the Norms and headed over to the observatory to greet Art and Dave.

The two gentlemen run the telescope for the nature center on every clear Friday night and remind me of kindly retreat masters or genial innkeepers, so welcoming are they in spirit to any and all who come to this sacred space. As Cathy and I peered into the doorway of the observatory, we could already see that they were occupied: Dave aligning the telescope on an object with a long line of would-be observers to his rear, Art busily answering the questions of another small group near the observatory work table and bookcase. This gave us an interval just to look at this remarkable enclosure. A curious phenomenon one immediately experiences upon entering such a small cylindrical space is that all sound travels in a circle, returning to itself, so that words uttered to one's left seemed to be heard also at the right. My eye fell on the red lights, strung out like an interior ribbon along the mid-wall of the entire observatory, familiar to me of course, since they enable an observer to log observations or consult star maps without destroying night vision; but tonight they spoke to me of something else I could not grasp at the moment.

But then … the telescope! In the middle of all the conversation quietly reposed the massive upturned instrument (a large refractor), designed to bring down fire from the sky—a fire that never was meant to be withheld from humanity. Gazing at it and the entire interior, as well as recalling my view of the observatory from afar, I mused on how natural it was that religion and astronomy were yokemates in the early history of the human race. This place was without doubt a temple, and its ongoing activities in large part acts of worship.

I asked a young man at the end of the line what he was going to see through the scope, and he responded, "A galaxy, I think." Right answer; for as I looked up in the direction of the tube, I saw clearly that it was aimed at the constellation Andromeda and its bright island universe, one of the showpieces of the autumn sky. I really wanted to see it, but the line was a bit too long at this point. I decided to come back later, but just then Art noticed me and came over. A kindly older gentleman, he greeted Cathy and me warmly. He was always doubly glad to see visitors who brought their own instruments to set up on the lawn adjoining the observatory; it gave people a chance to view sky wonders if the line before the great instrument was, as now, too long. We remarked that it looked to be a busy night and as we chatted, Dave, hearing my voice, smiled and waved. I would talk to him later too. Preparing to exit, I turned my eyes toward the roof opening for the telescope and again experienced the dance of enclosure and expanse—a vast swath of sky lay before my eyes, which we were viewing from a tiny circular house. Something about this and the red lights and the idea of temple were leading my spirit somewhere, but I didn't have it yet.

We exited and started toward the binoculars. I had already decided to begin with the Andromeda galaxy, since my appetite for it was not satiated at the big scope; but then I remembered there was even one more ritual I wanted to perform preparatory to observing. I told Cathy and the others I would be back in a minute, and walked out beyond the fence and a stand of trees at the back of the observatory lawn. Before me lay a vast sea of asphalt as far as the eye could see, somewhat dissonant with this bucolic setting but, considering its provenance, just as attractive, and a precious archaeological remnant to boot! Because of the darkness, I was sensing this vista as much as seeing it; but I had scanned it many times before during summer visits to Frosty Drew. Here was the actual takeoff and landing field of Charlestown Naval Air Station where in the 1940s future carrier pilots honed their skills before advancing to the Pacific theater and perhaps a quick end to a young life. Tarrying there for a moment longer I began to feel the vibes of World War II; in my mind's ear I tried to hear the whirring of aircraft engines, much as Dean Jagger did at the beginning of *Twelve O'Clock High* or Dana Andrews at the end of *The Best*

Years of Our Lives. My birth pre-dates—but just!—the end of the war, though two of my uncles served, and many men I knew during my lifetime saw action. A prayer of thanks is in order for their sacrifice; a rest-in-peace petition for those who suffered the numberless cruelties of that era; and, despite it all, a final recognition of the ecstasy of *that* time.

Back at the lawn, the binoculars were awaiting first light for the night. I looked high up in the east and, between the great quadrilateral of Pegasus, the winged horse, and the partially closed "umbrella" that is Perseus, I saw the constellation Andromeda, the chained lady, who mythology stipulates was rescued by what I have too easily dismissed as an "umbrella." The treasure that Andromeda hides is easily found—indeed, its existence was recorded as far back as AD 985—two stars out "left" (roughly northeast) from one of the corner stars of the great square of Pegasus, named Alpheratz, and another two stars "up" as one faces east, and the great galaxy is waiting. I adjusted the binoculars accordingly, and there it was: a great oval mass of white luminescence shining out large and bright against star points and blackness. A rotating island universe an impressive 110,000 light years across, the Andromeda Galaxy is situated an even more staggering 2.2 million light years from planet earth; yet astronomers classify it, as well as our own galactic home the Milky Way, as members of "the local group" (of galaxies), so matter-of-fact are they forced to be in describing distances contained within even larger spaces that could easily strike terror within the human heart.

I felt a tug at my elbow. Cathy was signaling that I was lingering too long at the eyecups; it was her turn. She peered in and exclaimed, "How beautiful!" as I felt a tremor of joy. I looked around at the Norms, Jan, Barbara, and Jerry; but they were all busy at their scopes. Waiting just behind Cathy, however, were a young woman and her daughter in patient anticipation. Cathy having finished, I didn't wait for them to ask; I quickly offered: "Would you like to see a galaxy?" The mother advanced first. I don't remember what I said to her—perhaps something about how far the Andromeda galaxy was from Earth; but she nodded appreciatively. Then her daughter moved forward, and the step stool was instantly produced. Her mother told her what she was about to see: a white oval spot that had as many stars in it as the rest of the night sky. The girl was silent for a minute, then shouted: "Oh, Mom, I see it!" The tremor broke out into gooseflesh. The child had said "yes" to the universe, and my body, by joining in the affirmation, made of it a prayer.

I peered into the binoculars again and savored the view. Doubtless, the images in the surrounding telescopes, and especially in the one inside the dome, were superior to the one I was looking at now—with moderate to high magnifications, the central core of the galaxy could be markedly differentiated from its diaphanous outer reaches. Binoculars, on the other hand, are typically confined to one low power. Yet they have one advantage over telescopes: two-eyed viewing. Observing this way gives one a sense of depth, almost of immersion in the object seen. As I continued to gaze, I recalled that the object—once called the Andromeda Nebula—was originally thought to be a congeries of glowing gases within our own galaxy. Its extra-galactic location and fully separate galactic status was only conclusively demonstrated in the 1920s by

The Andromeda Galaxy

the pioneering research of Edwin Hubble. Hints of the truth, however, were already strongly marked in the nineteenth century, prompting a French astronomer of that era, Camille Flammarion, to remark apropos of the dawning possibility of a cosmos infinitely larger than had been previously imagined, "The heavens are immense; man is insignificant!"

How to comment on such a breathtaking assertion: seven words that summarize centuries of agonized wondering in a pat formula? For my part, I can agree with Flammarion on the level of inchoate sentiment, but find myself resisting the hasty and somewhat depressing conclusion of his *obiter dictum*. Not that it can be without consolations: as religion's grip on the human imagination and its role in providing a framework for understanding the great questions have diminished in the modern era, scientists and some science writers, while always counseling humanity to makes its peace with a de-divinized universe, have sought to fill the consequent "enchantment deficit" out of science's own stock. Some have invited inquirers to take comfort in "being part of a great whole" or to discover joy in the realization that they are "stardust," that is, made of exactly the same stuff as the great lights that illuminate the night, just organized in a different way. The song "Circle of Life" from the Disney movie *The Lion King* is a variation of this fundamental theme, adapted for popular culture and with a focus on biological processes within the greater physical universe. I certainly am not averse to such thinking; it has an undoubted beauty and, more to the point, is true, if not (from where I sit) the whole truth. I say "not the whole truth" because I can't get out of my mind the words of the little girl as she beheld the Andromeda galaxy for the first time—"I see it"—and the notion that the galaxy, or Something, was ... waiting for such an utterance.

There is an emerging perspective on the universe which, while in no way endorsing or hinting at the validity of such high-blown speculations, is an incremental movement in their general direction. I am speaking of the so-called "anthropic principle": a theory or, better, a "posture for understanding" currently under discussion among practitioners of that branch of astronomy devoted to the study of the origin of the universe. Simply stated, it holds that the universe appears the way it does because we are here to see it. The proponents insist that contained within the content of questions about the nature of the universe—and therefore an issue that must be addressed concurrently if they are to be answered—is the fact that they are being asked at all. At its strongest, the theory stipulates that the universe demands life, even intelligent life, though not all scientists sympathetic to anthropic reasoning would subscribe to this quasi-philosophical modality of the theory. Still, the atmosphere here, whether weak or strong (thinkers associated with this theory sometimes refer to "weak" and "strong" anthropic reasoning), is decidedly un-Flammarionist.

The theory, of course, is not without severe critics within the scientific community, who claim that what we really have here is at best philosophy, at worst, sentimentality; and, while its advocates would vigorously challenge this assertion, they cannot claim to be offering science, for the hypothesis is in no way testable. Moreover, some scientists claim that theistic believers who are attracted to the anthropic principle because they see in it an emerging demonstration of the existence of

God have it completely wrong, that it points definitively in the opposite direction. Nevertheless, such believers will likely continue to be intrigued by the thesis and agree with one commentator who described the anthropic principle as a "dim awareness" that "haunts" cosmologists.

And what is haunting them? I think here of the ancient natural philosopher Archimedes, who, in demonstrating the mechanics of leverage, said, in effect, that if he had a lever long enough and a place to stand, he could lift the world. A possible inference from the anthropic principle is that human beings possess a kind of Archimedean platform—a separateness from all they perceive, even their bodies, even their own powers of perception—from which they are able to "know" and to "speak a word of assent," like the little girl, and, in so doing, "lift" galaxies to the completion of their being. Such thoughts are certainly repugnant to modern natural science which, so far as I can see, is more comfortable with variants of the "stardust hypothesis"—to wit, the universe has no subjunctive mood, no conditions contrary to or transcending fact. It is what it is and blindly does what it does, carrying along for the ride a humanity with a developed consciousness—helpful in the competition with other species, but also with a rather pathetic insistence on "meaning": a predilection that does not square with any facts and serves no apparent evolutionary purpose, but shows no sign of becoming the equivalent of a vestigial organ. A strange and anomalous byproduct of natural selection, indeed.

So, the issue is joined yet again. Anthropic principle (at least in its "haunting" sense) versus stardust hypothesis is simply the current incarnation of the great conversational transaction that has preoccupied all natural philosophy, all reasoned inquiry, all wonderment throughout history, in response to the enduring questions: What is Man? What, if anything, is important? Is there a Beyond beyond? They are the staple of the storied college bull session, where points made, leavened by too many beers, are more in the form of good-humored shots across the bows of each other's egos. I remember an opponent in one such joust, taking a long swig from a Bud, fixing me with a momentary stare, and then demolishing my whole evening's argumentation with one rhetorical swoop: "Maybe you're just a figment of my imagination!" Great fun? Of course. Not to be taken seriously? On the contrary: much depends on the answers to the questions embedded in such a throwaway line.

And the debate continues, likely without final resolution; yet, all human beings must somehow find an answer for themselves— one that will emerge from simply living, if it is not attended to discursively. I probably have done as much thinking about the issue as the average person; and though my education in philosophy has huge gaps and is fairly shallow in most places, I have been an interested observer of the journey out from Socrates to Sartre and back from Buber to the Buddha, with occasional side trips into literature and science. From all this experience, I have come to one principle that seems to me incontestable in the final analysis: "Things don't really matter if matter is the only thing." And I really mean "really"—not in the "reduced to practical consequences" sense in which it is most often used ("We have been arguing all day about what is the best cuisine, but what do you *really* want for dinner?"), but rather in its primary definition of "as pertains to the real" or "having objective existence." And by the second "matter," I don't just refer to matter, but to energy as well—and to dark matter, dark energy, the entire content of parallel universes, if any, and/or to the whole of the many dimensional but possibly crumbled and compactified universe that is hypothesized in the string theory of modern physics.

In the face of all this, and wholly independent of it, is the human insistence on "mattering." The killer angel, it appears, can live under no other aspect; cannot do without organizing facts so that they reveal a higher order called "meaning." That is why they hold memorial services for, build monuments to, and write obituaries about people, even those who may have spent their whole lives trying to prove that "remembering" itself is a mere flutter of synapses in the cerebral cortex. Because human lives "matter" and are not just matter, or so it seems to me. And thus it is that I find myself in my mind's eye standing side by side with Camille Flammarion, gazing at the Andromeda galaxy and feeling the same awe and sense of human diminishment. Yet something at my ear is whispering thoughts that prevent me from reaching the Flammarionist conclusion. Instead, my final disposition completes a circle that includes self-regard as well as veneration: the universe is no greater than my sense of wonder at it; I am as large inside.

More people were arriving, but for the moment there was no one standing in line at my binoculars. I sensed that unless I wanted to spend the rest of the evening observing the Andromeda galaxy—not a wholly unattractive idea—it would be a good time to move on to another object. I adjusted the binoculars northward to Perseus again, then moved above the apex star in the "umbrella," called Merkib by some, toward the constellation Cassiopeia. Without much difficulty I located the magnificent starfield known as the Double Cluster—perhaps seven hundred stars in a span of one degree, with two concentration areas that appear to be colliding. Over seventy light years across and eight thousand light years distant, the Double Cluster was identified as a "cloudy spot" by Ptolemy and other ancients, though they could not have imagined it was situated in another spiral arm of the galaxy the Earth calls home.

After I savored the view for long seconds, Cathy took her turn, and then the Norms and Jerry, whom I had hailed. The Double Cluster is a fine object in a telescope also, but it requires low-power eyepieces to be seen to good effect; this is one kind of stellar apparition where binoculars are not at that much of a disadvantage. There were appreciative nods all around, as some of the new arrivals queued up. Then the joy of waiting for reactions and listening for responses. There were plenty of "oohs," "aahs," "oh wows," and more than a smattering of the dreaded "cool!"—all of which was music to my soul, and gooseflesh to my body.

Then the petitioners for a look melted away as quickly as they had coagulated, giving me a chance to change to yet another object. What next? Since my binoculars were already in the vicinity, I thought I would try to find a lovely little asterism that had become a favorite. Asterisms are groupings of stars that are smaller than the recognized constellations but memorable enough to have achieved a sort of standard reference on their own. The greatest of them all is the Big Dipper, not a constellation but only part of one: the hindquarters and tail of the Great Bear. Others include the "circlet" in Pisces, the "great square" of Pegasus, and the "sickle" of Leo (the Lion). The asterisms that interest me, however, are those whose discovery requires optical aid, and for the finding of which, binoculars, with their wide field views, particularly excel. Waiting to be revealed all over the sky are assorted houses, arrows, golf putters, coat hangers, engagement rings, and other miscellaneous articles of natural and artificial origin.

My search on this occasion was for Kemble's Cascade, a "waterfall" of eight-magnitude stars hidden away in the constellation Camelopardalis (the Giraffe) and named for the Canadian Franciscan friar and astronomer who took significant note of it. It took a bit longer to find than the Double Cluster, but I eventually had it centered, occupying just about the entire field of view of the binoculars. After locking the tripod azimuth knob, I looked around and there were the mother and daughter who had visited earlier for Andromeda. I told them what they were about to see, and then for some reason held my breath as the child peered in. "I see it, I see it," she exclaimed. Those words again! They touched off a renewed outbreak of gooseflesh; the words I then realized I had been waiting for.

As I slowly exhaled, a verse of scripture from the King James Bible offered itself for my contemplation, as it so often does under these circumstances: "Now we see through a glass, darkly ... " The words of St. Paul from his first letter to the Corinthians—one of the loveliest chapters in the Bible, perhaps the greatest encomium to Love in the history of literature. The phrase that came to mind is actually the first term in a sequence of contrasting perspectives, followed by "... but then, face to face.": the import being that our vision of eternal things is much impaired on this side of life ("through a glass, darkly"), but that in the life beyond it will be much improved ("face to face"). All this, of course, is lost in the rogue exegesis, which I am coming more and more to specialize in; for to me it seems that here and now, at Frosty Drew in the dark, and aided by optical instruments— the divine "glass"—our seeing of the Eternal is far from impaired. It is clearer than at most other times and cannot be substantially different from—dare I say it?—visions to come.

The Norms approached. Did I want to go into the observatory for a look in the big scope if the line was not too long? Yes, it was time again. Cath, who had already been back to the observatory a couple of times since our first visit of the evening, agreed to be in charge of the binoculars for the few remaining people wanting to see Kemble's Cascade. As the Norms and I came near the doorway to the great dome, I was almost inclined to genuflect—the feeling that I was entering a temple or church strongly affecting me once again. The great scope was two-thirds or more elevated from the horizon, but this time in the western sky. I got into the moderately sized line immediately, while the Norms held back and then briefly exited as someone called out to them.

As I neared the eyepiece, I saw that the telescope was pointed at the constellation Lyra, the Harp—a charming little parallelogram of stars with two additional points of light, one of which is the brilliant first-magnitude, blue-white star named Vega. Associated variously in lore and mythology with the harp of Orpheus, Hermes, Apollo, or King David,

Lyra is a summer constellation but was now headed to its western obscurity at the behest of autumnal star groupings. The bespectacled Dave, explaining to each viewer what he or she was seeing, paused for a moment to look up and was greeted by my three-word question: "The Smoke Ring?" He nodded appreciatively as I finally reached the eyepiece and peered in to see a delicate circular white apparition, magnified one-hundred-plus times, looking uncannily like a ring just exhaled from a cigar smoker's mouth.

The "Smoke Ring" or Ring Nebula, number 57 in Monsieur Messier's catalogue of deep space comet imposters, is a "planetary" nebula: the glowing entrails of a dying star but with a perceptibly rounded shape, to be distinguished from its relatively formless cousins known as "diffuse" nebulae. Enjoying the detail of the image, I recalled how difficult an object the Smoke Ring is for smaller telescopes or binoculars—primarily due to its small angular size and low surface brightness. Sometimes, when trying to find it with my own modest instrument at very low power, I have "seen" it primarily because I knew it was there. I mused at how this is a personal recapitulation of the age old chicken/egg question of where knowledge begins—perception or innate ideas—that has dogged epistemologists down the centuries. What light might this experience throw on the dynamics of the spiritual journey? I quickly snapped out of my reverie; I could hear Cathy's voice in my mind telling me I was lingering too long at the eyepiece. I said a hasty "nice view" to Dave and dismounted the observing platform, noting that the line had considerably lengthened in the interim. There at the end with rueful smiles were the Norms, their temporary departure from the observatory costing them dearly in the matter of expeditious advancement to the telescope's eyepiece.

I decided to wait for them, a lingering sentiment overtaking me akin to the one I had experienced on my first visit to the observatory that evening. I looked back up to the pleasing panorama of sky contained window-like by the dome's opening, and then, my head lowering, my eyes fell again on the red lights, faithful friend of the astronomer's night vision. In an instant, it hit me. The red lights! In my religion, red light—the sanctuary lamp—signals the presence of God. My thoughts began to roll. I meditated on how curious it was that the sacred architecture and liturgy of biblical religion, Judaic and Christian—even keeping in mind outsized enclosures like Gothic cathedrals—marked the advance to the locus of the divine as a journey to smaller and smaller spaces. There was David's temple in Jerusalem, within which were various courts signaling ritualistic affinity to the family of God, within which was the Holy of Holies, behind a veil of which was the Ark of the Covenant, within which were the tablets of the Law containing the animating presence of God. Similarly, in the Catholic/Orthodox/Anglican tradition, there are churches, within which are sanctuaries—spaces heretofore separated by a rail, within which are tabernacles, inside of which are *ciboria*, containing within the Host—the very Divinity that shaped the cosmos.

My mind veered for a second to my youth and the delight I took in my mother's set of canisters: flour, sugar, coffee, tea. They were a staple in kitchens in the fifties—the cylindrically-shaped ones crafted to contain each other—small to large—if not in use. Advancing to the Holy of Holies, to the tabernacle, had that same sense of delight as of removing canisters one after another when my mother allowed me to play with them. Would there be a treasure at the end? It was always my hope. The observatory, I thought, is not unlike a canister, an ark, a tabernacle; but here it is *we* who are contained inside and— the red lights giving ever faithful witness, only this time in the inverse—God who is spread abroad in those vast spaces. I looked around at the telescope, probing for His footfall in a remote corner of the universe, and then again at the lights. It was like worshiping—in the vernacular of Catholicism, "paying a visit to the tabernacle"—only using the right side of the brain.

The Norms having finally looked through the scope, we decided to return to our wives and astronomical instruments. Immediately outside the door of the observatory, I almost collided with some younger children doing cartwheels. Realizing that it was indeed a long and a late night for these young ones, I was still momentarily irritated, then fearful for my binoculars, perilously mounted on a high tripod. Something inside me told me immediately that it was all right, and that if children were playing, properly supervised of course, well, that was maybe more than all right. Walking across the lawn, I was struck by how clearly I could recognize the faces of people without the benefit of artificial light. I was seeing by starlight!—under the aegis of which everyone is kin and no one a stranger.

There was animation near my binoculars. I could see Cathy, Barbara, and Janice talking to a tall bearded figure with large dense hair and a radiant smile with which he seemed to embrace the world. It could easily be Jesus, but it was Ray—an embodiment of the principle that in Rhode Island you are very likely to be related to a person in at least two ways. Ray is Cathy's second cousin and, quite independently, a close friend of my sister's, with whom he shares a passion for photography. Ray greeted me and the Norms with a hug but almost immediately switched gears; as a late arriving pilgrim, he was anxious to get down to business. "What are we looking at tonight?" he asked, it seemed, to me.

My first impulse was, as always, to look northeast; and there, having by now cleared the observatory dome with a large space of sky to spare, was a stellar apparition to delight Ray and our entire company of sky suppliants, as it had our ancestors from time out of mind. The Pleiades—the most famous star cluster in the heavens, the asterism of asterisms, known and commented upon as far back as the third millennium BC and mentioned in holy scripture—had arisen. A compact little group of six or seven stars, looking like a little dipper for which it is sometimes mistaken, it discloses ten times that many with even modest optical aid; and with larger instruments, reveals a silver braid of nebulosity enveloping its stars.

The Pleiades was a sure winner at an observing night such as this, so I quickly switched the binoculars in its direction and locked down the azimuth knob. The view was stunning. The six principal stars that framed the "dipper" were now filled in with points of light in cascades and streamers; I could barely contain a joyful response but held my peace to savor the reactions of those to follow in line, especially the one right behind me: Ray. He advanced to the eyecups, settled his pupils comfortably in

The Pleiades

them, and then … a highly audible intake of breath followed by wordlessness. Here was another experience in the inverse: my music teacher friend exhaled when we had shared the joy of a concert piece; now Ray's delight in the cosmos produced a reciprocal signal from his life's breath. It was as if he were trying to inhale the divine effulgence emanating from this starry masterpiece; the Holy Ghost at the speed of light!

The Pleiades is another one of those celestial objects where the view in binoculars can rival that of small telescopes, so that I noted that even the Norms were waiting to look before returning to their instruments. Indeed, there was now a fairly long line; I would be needed only to adjust the binoculars from time to time as the rotation of the Earth nudged the star grouping from the field. Meanwhile, I would eagerly wait as fresh observers voiced their responses, and hope for the gooseflesh they might produce; the gooseflesh from Ray's gasp was only now just dying down.

I sensed that the evening would shortly come to a close. Though there were many regular visitors and astronomy enthusiasts who kept Art and Dave on duty into the wee hours, our group, facing a late-night journey home of an hour or more, would not be among them. It was getting a bit cold. An older man looking into the binoculars said, "Oh, wow!" I turned to listen to his joy and exchange a few words, then looked back at the observatory where people were going in and out. How to sum up this evening?

My spirit embraced a passage from that most mystical of Gospels: St. John's. In the tenth chapter, Jesus describes himself as the

Good Shepherd in an extended allegory/story full of interesting ambiguities and sidelights, not the least of which is an abrupt change in focus. Where in the beginning, He identifies himself as the kindly and dependable shepherd, whose voice the sheep recognize, He becomes in the second part of the story—or really the second story—the actual gate through which they pass to safety. In the matter of sidelights, there is the mysterious "keeper" or "porter" who opens the gate for the shepherd—I remember a philosophy professor insisting once that here was an understated allegory of the Holy Spirit—and again, there is the unforgettable pronouncement of Jesus—"Other sheep have I which are not of this fold; them too I must bring, that there may be one flock, one shepherd" —fraught with such pleasing ecumenical, interfaith, and world-unifying implications.

Predictably, none of these was my focus; instead I was most interested in the actual sheepfold itself and the surrounding pasture. Enclosure ... and expanse. Which one is the desirable place to be, which more a picture of heaven? In the first part of the story, there is the sense that the sheep are penned up (in this world?), waiting for the good shepherd to arrive and "lead them out" (to heavenly open spaces?). Later, when Jesus describes himself as the "gate," it appears that the sheep (the human soul) is trying to get in to safe haven from a wide world of marauding wolves. In the end, the story strikes a comforting equivocal note on this issue: the soul who has identified the genuine shepherd, who has found the Truth, "will go in and out and find pasture."

"Going in and going out"—of the observatory, that is—that is what struck me most about the evening. As some people were lined up at my binoculars to see the Pleiades, others were entering the dome, and still others exiting. Meanwhile, the younger members of this nocturnal flock were engaged in games of tag and hide-and-go-seek—*homo ludens*—"man at play." Their seniors were playing too—whether in the observatory or on the green—frolicking in the star fields of the Milky Way, finding eternal soul-pasture.

It occurred to me that this is what a night in the Primordial Garden might have looked like—Frosty Drew as Eden. Indeed, the words "I see it" and their innumerable variants uttered this night when eye met galaxy—why, they are already part of the music of the heavenly choir that, it is said, unceasingly attends God's throne.

(VII)

CUM MORTUIS

"Gray hair is a crown of glory." Proverbs 16:31

"The souls of the just are in the hand of God.
 They seemed in the view of the foolish to be dead;
 but they are in peace." Wisdom 3:1–3

"And also with you." The old woman's greeting, tendered to my back after I had moved a few paces away from her, brought me up short and at the same time shattered my presumption. I had just offered her the sign of peace: "Peace be with you," the ritual immediately preceding the "Lamb of God" in the Roman Catholic liturgy, but had not expected the designated response. Why? Because she was a resident of an Alzheimer's unit in a nursing home and had been staring impassively into space for the last twenty minutes, or so I thought.

For more than ten years on alternate Saturdays it was in a nursing home that I found myself—a commandeered but cheerful assistant to Deacon Al, a good man with a title that needs explanation. "Deacon" refers to a person who has varying responsibilities in different Christian denominations; but in the Roman Catholic tradition a deacon is a clergyman, empowered to preside at certain rituals, including baptism and burial services; to serve Mass as a vested assistant to the priest; and to preach in liturgical settings. The diaconate, which began in the New Testament as a ministry of charity, gradually evolved in the Middle Ages to a post of high church administration (Gregory I was an archdeacon immediately before his elevation to the papacy), and in more recent years in the Catholic Church was more or less a sacramentally transitional phase for those advancing to priesthood.

Of the many reforms of the Second Vatican Council (1962–1965) that reshaped the contours of Catholic life, one was the revival of the permanent diaconate—a clerical state to which both celibate and married men (Al has a wife and three children) can be called. The intentions of the Holy Spirit in this matter are of course never to be fully discerned; yet one thing is abundantly clear: the number of priests has declined precipitously in recent years, forcing those who have continued to serve to narrow the amplitude of their activities in many cases. To fill this gap, the laity and deacons are now performing a variety of ministries; and deacons, because of their status as ordained persons, can bring to those who are immobile or confined for one reason or another the flavor of the Catholic liturgy.

One of these places of confinement is a nursing home—Al's choice for a ministry setting, and by extension, that of his assistants. They are mostly women, who, as always, do some of the heaviest lifting in the Church's ongoing labor of salvation.

I was one of the few men he successfully drafted—with a large hand on my shoulder and a straightforward appeal emanating from a deeply tanned face (Al had been a building contractor for years). What I volunteered for was a Saturday afternoon regimen that unfolded as follows: Al and those of us who assisted him would arrive at the nursing home and meet in a large community room on the second floor, at one end of which was a makeshift altar. After greeting each other and briefly socializing, we would fan out to the entire building to transport patients in wheelchairs or to assist those walking to the room. When everyone was assembled, Al would conduct a communion service, sometimes with music, and with the assistance of the volunteers. The communion service is not Mass; being a deacon, Al could not consecrate the host as a priest would. Rather, he would bring already-consecrated hosts from our parish to be distributed at the appropriate time. In other respects, the service looked very much like a Mass: There were ritual prayers, readings from scripture, a homily or sermon, the Lord's Prayer, and communion. The astute among the attending residents realized that it was not the Mass; yet, a service with many familiar rites, over which presided a vested clergyman, plugged a deep hole in their sensibilities that was left when entry into the nursing home made church attendance difficult and, for some, impossible.

After the service, the volunteers would wheel or escort the residents back to their rooms and then reassemble in the community room, from whence they again dispersed to perform one of two ministries. Some would bring the sacrament to those who, for one reason or another, were confined to their rooms or beds, celebrating with these patients the brief ritual of communion for the sick. Others accompanied Al to the third floor of the home, where he presided at a second modified service for residents in the Alzheimer's unit. For a while I served in the former capacity but eventually gravitated exclusively to the latter.

It is a consciousness-altering experience to assist in a group activity with those suffering the long good-bye of this insidious disease. The temptation is to become numb to the patients' routine inability to participate meaningfully in the service, to resolve to go through the motions and get it over with in the face of what appears to be their failure to comprehend what once may have been dear to them. The fabric of such assumptions is quickly left in tatters, however, by persons who will not be dismissed that easily, like an old woman returning in perfect diction the formula of the Rite of Peace—"And also with you"—to a blasé volunteer with one eye on the clock and his mind on the evening's activities to come.

Having been granted an epiphany, I decided there and then to "turn aside" and investigate more of this burning bush—God speaking to me clearly from the mental faculties of those for whom clarity was an almost totally diminished asset. I began to relish this part of my nursing home service the most, not least because it was I who was the object of ministry, I came to realize. I was impressed nearly every week by the power of the liturgy, with its plenitude of gestures and ritual spoken responses—the sign of the cross, bowings, genuflections, elevations, the "Lord, have mercy," the "Lamb of God"—to spark recognition in the fading embers of memory. At times I thought I perceived among the residents—as grace empowered a declining nature—an almost superhuman effort to retrieve the last remaining ounce of concentrated attentiveness available from irreversibly deteriorating brain tissue for the task of celebrating the great Mystery. One such experience, I warrant, would give pause to anyone attached to facile nostrums about these individuals' lack of quality of life.

It was actually quite surprising that it took so long for me to grasp the possibilities of ministry to the elderly and those of their number needing special attention. The truth is that I have had an affinity for the aged since my boyhood. My older brother used to make fun of how I "bowed and scraped" to my great aunts Lucy, Kate, and Mabel—daughters of Charles Pierce and sisters of my grandmother. I couldn't grasp his point or appreciate his humor. Didn't he see that my behavior was a proper response to people who bore within their own flesh the treasure of our family history, and whose countenances were accordingly backlit like the trees of an October sunset? Another experience involved the grey eminence of our dead-end street—a retired semi-professional magician named Charles Fenner—who lived in a diminutive abode next to our three-decker. At one point he took a few of us boys in and showed us how to perform magic. Mr. Fenner, bearer of a distinguished surname in Rhode Island history, was a devotee of beauty and grace, introducing us, long before we had it in school, to an appreciation of the performing arts, especially music. He was a classic example of how much young people, if they are willing to listen, can learn from one who has lived a long life.

During my "hidden years"—after college and the military—when I was trying to figure out how I wanted to spend my life, I tried a number of non-lucrative jobs and positions. Naturally, one of them involved the aged: I answered a newspaper advertisement for an orderly in a nursing home/convalescent hospital. During the six months that I worked there I steadily lost weight; and when it was time to move on, I was but a shadow of my former self—not that hefty to begin with. My job primarily consisted of a morning round of helping patients out of bed; assisting a number of the elderly males with personal care tasks; helping patients with their meals when the nursing assistants were short-staffed; returning a goodly number to bed after lunch; and getting them out of bed again just before my shift ended. It was a grueling regimen, and not long after beginning employment I began to doubt the justice and proportionality of my pay when weighed against my work output. I continue to believe that the wages of those who toil in nursing homes is a national scandal.

It was about that time that I discovered my employment was rewarding according to a different pay scale. My thoughts would sometimes move on from an unproductive fixation on my own low compensation to what my activities were like for those on the receiving end. A daily routine of excavating one's body from perhaps a troubled sleep with the assistance of a paid staff whose moods might vary from day to day, only to be returned thereto and compelled to do it again before the setting sun brought a temporary and partial surcease—this was living? Yes it was, for the many—though certainly not all—who were the objects of my ministrations. I sometimes sensed, when my eyes met theirs, a serenity, an acceptance, a divine resignation about the reduced circumstances of their lives that made my services necessary but in turn allowed me to experience the peculiar grace that I believe surrounds the aged.

A noteworthy instance of this in my own brief employed tenure in the nursing home field was that of an elderly woman whom I had to lift, under the watchful eye of a private-duty nurse, onto the toilet several times a shift. The lady had been a distinguished churchwoman in the United Church of Christ and a professor at the Hartford Seminary. A world traveler, she was also a published author—one of her books graces my shelves and is a possession I hold dear. When I met her, however, the woman was suffering from advanced dementia, alternately staring into space and then rousing herself to offer bits of incoherent verbiage. On my first attempt to lift her she gripped my forearms so tightly I thought I would scream; but it was she who did the screaming. Gradually, it got easier, as she recognized me and our facial expressions became a medium of communication upon which was built what I can only call a relationship. My question is: who can be sure that this passage in her life—judged under the aspect of eternity—is less important than her church work, teaching, and publications? The answer: only a worldly vision that accounts such medallions of success as determinative in weighing a life in the balance, but of which God might say, "My thoughts are not your thoughts."

One aspect of my attraction to the elderly that I reflected on for years but ultimately put to rest was what this tendency said about my own psychological development. When I used to tell friends about my strong attraction to the old, in one or two cases they suggested that it might arise from an unresolved authority or parental displacement issue. Some of this might be dismissed as dime-store psychoanalysis, of which there are, for my money, far too many practitioners on this planet. In a similar vein, this kind of rapid-fire categorization might label those who enjoy working with teenagers as people trying to relive their adolescence. Still when allowance is made for such superficiality, I had to admit that some of these comments came my way from persons of proven insight. My response is to accede to the possible or even probable truth of their conclusions but to assert that it is unproductive to dwell for long thereon. The human journey is a complex dance of physical and psychical movements intertwined with divine activity, the frontiers of which are sometimes hard to discern. That is why I believe that my affinity for the aged—whatever it says about my psychological maturity or lack thereof—is also a gift from God that I was meant somehow to give in turn.

It is not as easy to tie up into such a neat explanatory bundle my prevailing attitude toward those with whom, in my mind, the elderly are closely associated—namely, the dead. Older people to whom I have been unguarded enough to reveal this perspective have, naturally, reacted with strong exception, often followed by verbal reprimands. And my cavalier and copiously stated philosophy of death—a kind of lighthearted dismissal of all the fuss and fear, coupled with a joyous anticipation of my own going forth—has understandably deeply offended many persons, especially those closest to me. This takes a bit of explanation.

There is nothing in human life as certain as death and taxes, says Ben Franklin—an adage, the humor of which everyone instantly grasps and appreciates. The saying achieves this end by deploying a species of hyperbole: death, universally dreaded, is part of the irreducible existential landscape of mankind; taxes, also onerous, are a human artifice that in principle need not have been. To confer upon them, even fleetingly, a kind of metaphysical equivalence is of course nonsense, but works to reveal the depth of the worldwide resentment of the unavoidability of taxation and the tax man. Franklin's *bon mot,* however, is disarmed of its meaning for the likes of me, as will become clear below.

Religion sometimes calls forth a benign analogy for death such as "falling asleep," but much more often gives specific and often metaphorical utterance to the view that is a sub-text in Franklin's witticism. Death is the all-pervading reality that haunts mankind in every waking moment—a void, a crevasse, a black gap between time and eternity, a long journey that at the very least is fraught with hazards. It can be faced and even faced down—but this requires every virtue that humankind can assemble and consistently apply, plus for many, if not most, faith systems, a generous outpouring of supernatural aid. The Catholic tradition, for instance, has regarded the stakes involved at the moment of death to be so high that it literally bombards those about to depart with a maximum dose of sacramental grace. In the so-called "last rites," the dying person may receive the anointing of the sick, penance, and communion under its name specific to the occasion— "Viaticum" or, loosely translated, "something for the way," the implication being that divine sustenance is required for the uncertain voyage about to be undertaken. Such an odyssey is most often symbolized in religious literature as the crossing of a great water barrier—an ocean or sea (perhaps most famously the Red Sea) or, as the American spiritual has it, a deep river that the hopeful journeyer, under grace, must ford to arrive at the felicitous "campground."

Against the shores of my consciousness, this near-universal sentiment of religion and age-old wisdom washes ceaselessly but in vain. To me, death is but a thin membrane separating those who have crossed over from those who remain in this life. That is why I associate so readily the old with the dead: it is not that the old seem almost dead to me—the inference that my elderly interlocutors most often draw and take exception to—but simply that the dead seem like my seniors: living on, continuing to be themselves, always accessible through prayer and reminiscence.

No one has to remind me that such a view could be characterized as false bravado, a kind of whistling past the graveyard, and at worst, a strategy of denial of perhaps the most basic reality attending the human condition. More than my affinity for the old, it is this attitude toward the dead that might not bear the psychologist's scrutiny. And when it is also discovered that I am not at present facing my own death or those of my closest loved ones, my critics could rightly comment that when those eventualities occur—as they must—I will likely be singing a different tune. The funny thing is that, although I hold fast to my minimalist view of death, it is not as if I have not witnessed firsthand its power and mystery.

Two incidents surrounding two different deaths have instructed me as to the numinous power of the great departure. Once Cathy and I visited in the hospital an elderly friend who was not expected to live more than a few days. He had lost his faculty of swallowing and was receiving nourishment and fluids intravenously. His mouth understandably quite dry, he kept asking for water, and Cathy in response lubricated his lips with a sponge-like swab attached to a short rod. When I related this story to my sister, she instantly compared it to the dying Christ, who was likewise plagued by thirst. As the great Catholic theologian Karl Rahner and others have noted, in the Christian faith, every act of dying is a dying with Christ—that is, somehow through, with, and in the individual's dying we behold again the death of Christ. In this case our friend became for a moment the Christ of "I thirst," and Cathy stood in the place of that nameless person who attempted to give relief to the Suffering Servant. I will never read the Passion narrative of St. John quite the same way again.

Another incident several years ago involved my older brother, who at the time was in declining health but not thought to be in imminent danger of death. Suddenly, a few days before Christmas, I received a call that he had had a heart attack and had not survived. The following day, just after I had returned home from conferring with my sister about funeral arrangements, I received another phone call. At first, I could barely make out any words; the person on the other end of the line was obviously struggling with every syllable. Then I realized it was my father-in-law, stricken for months with lung cancer and rapidly failing. He assured me in a tremulous, pianissimo voice that he would be praying for the repose of the soul of my brother Ken! These were the last words he ever spoke to me; the day after Christmas he too died.

It is perhaps this second experience that has confirmed in me a stance of equivocation about the reality of death. I cannot deny that the process of dying is suffused with pain and suffering, mystery, and high drama: all the literature and symbolizations of the human community testify to it. My father-in-law's decision, even in his terribly diminished condition, to pray for my brother is a striking confirmation. But it also gives witness to another truth to which I hold fast—the kinship between the living and the dead, especially close between those who are immediately on either side of that which I insist on calling a "thin membrane." Reflecting on all this, I would have to say that the final word for me on the subject of death is best encapsulated by using again the time-honored metaphor of the river crossing—a river that for me is deep, certainly; just not wide.

Unlike my attitude to the elderly, which appears to have been bred in the bone, my strongly marked ideas about death (bracketing off for the moment the credo of my religion, which many of us repeat—"I believe in the Resurrection … "—but do not always internalize) I trace to a singular experience. It occurred in Italy during my service time in the Air Force. I had been assigned to do a tour of duty at a small base near the city of Brindisi in Apulia—the heel of the boot on the Adriatic coast. My job specialty was communications security—an enterprise that had to proceed twenty-four hours a day. As a consequence, there were four groups of servicemen assigned: *Abel*, *Baker*, *Charlie*, and *Dog* flights (In the army they have platoons and companies; in the Air Force, flights and squadrons). To accommodate the all-day coverage, one flight would work one of the three shifts of the day—7:00 AM to 4:00 PM; 4:00 PM to midnight; and midnight to 7:00 AM—while one flight would be off. The rotational schedule worked like this: a flight would enter its work cycle on the swing shift, 4:00 PM to midnight; work four days; get twenty-four hours off; work four midnight-to-7:00 AM shifts; get twenty-four hours off; work four 7:00 AM-to-4:00 PM shifts; get four twenty-four hour periods off (i.e., from 4:00 PM of the last day shift to 4:00 PM of the first swing shift). Variations of such odd work cycles are common in the military. The down-side of this one was managing the sleep-time transitions inherent in rotating shifts; failure to do so could—and often did—bring biorhythmic disaster; the up-side, as I saw it, was that the extended break offered chances to travel farther afield than a normal weekend.

I didn't miss the opportunities; in fact, I eventually had making the most of them down to a science. My bags were already packed on the fourth day of the day shift so that, quickly emerging from the duty compound, I need only grab my satchel and catch the bus into town to board the 5:04 PM train departing Brindisi and climbing the spine of Italy to points north, with an eventual terminus in Munich. My second-class ticket in hand, I soon became one of the "sardines" on these overloaded conveyances, packed with whole families traveling to visit their men—husbands, sons, fathers—many of whom were working in Germany where the jobs were more plentiful. Beginning with this train, armed with connecting schedules, and the beneficiary of a four-day pass, I was able to travel to Munich, Vienna, Geneva, and Heidelberg—not to mention more proximate Italian destinations such as Florence and Venice.

That was in the somewhat misty future as I arrived at the base in mid-March in the late sixties with a couple of tech-school buddies. After a brief orientation, we joined *Baker* Flight on the first swing shift. Having realized the possibilities my work cycle held for traveling, I was busy thinking about destinations, but had no plans to go anywhere on my first break. Then suddenly I decided that I couldn't pass up the chance; I would only get so many. I also knew where I wanted to go first: Rome! My preparations were hasty—I was not yet at the peak form I would be in six months—but during my off-duty hours I managed to check train schedules and make arrangements to convert my dollars into lire. There were no takers to join me; my buddies were too new to the base and I had not gotten to know others well enough. So I went alone.

Taking a late-evening train after the last swing shift, I would try to sleep in my second-class accommodations, with only an interruption to switch trains in Bari, Foggia, or Pescara—I don't remember which. I arrived in Rome in the early morning with absolutely no plan of what to do (later I would use a generously dog-eared copy of Arthur Frommer's *Europe on Five Dollars a Day*) and even less than tourist-book Italian. Emerging from the station, I scanned a bank of waiting taxis and impulsively called out to an unencumbered cab driver one of the few Italian place names I knew, "Piazza San Pietro." Seconds later, it seemed to me—Italian taxis travel at something just less than the speed of light—I got my first sight of the massive dome of the cathedral, and was unceremoniously let out at the perimeter of St. Peter's Square. My awestruck mood quickly passed as I realized that, before I could savor any of the beauties of the Eternal City, I would have to find a place to stay. As luck would have it, there was a USO in the immediate vicinity, with a staff ever ready to help a serviceman in need. But as I told one of the service personnel my requirements, she shook her head while relating that there was not a vacant room to be had in Rome on Holy Saturday. At this point in my life I had traveled so far from my faith that I had lost all track of liturgical seasons—I had arrived in Rome without a reservation on Easter Weekend!

Dejected, I turned to leave when she grabbed my arm—her list of cancellations, apparently updated hourly, yielded an opening at the Pensione Risorgimento just down the street. Minutes later I was settled in modest but commodious quarters, and soon after that taking meals with people I didn't know but learned to like immensely despite the language barrier. I even had time that day to take in some very local sites, such as the Piazza Navona and Hadrian's tomb. Easter Sunday found me in St. Peter's Square to receive the papal blessing with a jostling multinational throng, and later touring St. Peter's and waiting endlessly for admittance to the Sistine Chapel. Monday, my last day, the USO staffer had booked me for a tour of some sites more remote than walking distance: the baths of Caracalla, St. Paul's Outside the Walls, and the catacombs of San Domitilla on the ancient Via Ardeatina.

At the catacombs, the tour participants were shepherded into a large subterranean chamber where the guide began an interesting but somewhat overlong discourse on this, the meeting place of the early Christians. He was pointing out what looked to be a primitive stone altar when I found my attention beginning to falter; the emotional ups and downs of the weekend, the lack of restful sleep, the drive to pack as much sightseeing as possible into this three-day window of opportunity, were at last beginning to show. I was roused only when we were directed out of the chamber single-file down a narrow corridor. I remember looking up at the paltry light bulbs providing dim illumination to our steps before we stopped and assembled in a semi-circle around a small, eye-level, much-worn cave painting. I noted that it was a rendering of the Virgin and child only an instant before the guide triumphantly announced it, launching into another disquisition as my attention began again slowly to wane.

I found myself re-engaged just as he was saying: "Doubtless this proves how early in Christian history devotion to the Madonna emerged." This caught my attention, since when I was a boy, Mary (the woman of faith) had been a bone of contention in arguments among my relatives, a mixture of Protestants and Catholics. Back in the bad old days before the ecumenical spirit, Protestant-Catholic animus was common; and I remember vividly the tension that attended weddings in my family when the Protestant contingent would have to enter a Catholic church, or vice versa. Meditating briefly on this primitive artwork, I thought for the first time how regrettable it was that Christians had allowed differences over what does and does not constitute a worthy object of veneration to sunder the peace of the cave of Bethlehem, to intrude on the joy of a mother and her delight in an infant, whatever her theological status.

The guide spoke on and my mind wandered again. My attention gravitated toward the left and behind, where there was another corridor perpendicular to the one we occupied; however, here there were no ceiling light bulbs; just a terrifying blackness. It occurred to me, remembering what the guide had mentioned at the beginning, that the early Christians met in the catacombs because they were subterranean burial places and sacrosanct in

Roman law and custom—an important consideration in eras of persecution. Suddenly the significance of the catacombs as Christian antiquities was replaced in my mind by the thought that here in this unlit void were interred the remains of persons whose names are now lost to history—not the Caesars and Ciceros, but ordinary Romans who married and worked hard to earn a living, raised children, and grew old gracefully—just like my father.

My father! He had died earlier in the decade; and now images of him came crowding into my consciousness, along with something else: music. After a few seconds of trying to grasp the theme, I recognized it as "Promenade" from Mussorgsky's *Pictures at an Exhibition*. "Promenade" is the musical connective tissue of this piano turned orchestral suite, describing the strolling interims between the observer's inspection of different paintings, musical descriptions of which constitute the individual movements of the piece. At the end, however, the composer puts "Promenade" into the minor mode for a picture entitled *Catacombae, Sepulcrum Romanum; Cum Mortuis in Lingua Mortua* (roughly, "The Catacombs, a Roman Sepulcher; With the Dead in a Dead Language"—the painting depicted a man examining skulls in a subterranean chamber).

The eerie musical thematic seemed entirely appropriate for the mood that overtook me. The chilling thought that offered itself from this black corridor was that my father's being was traveling the road to oblivion, pioneered by those who had been laid to rest here. I of course remembered him, albeit more indistinctly every day; but those who came after me and the ones who came after them would have less and less of a sense of him until he was extinguished—swallowed up, like all the un-famous dead, into a black hole where the memory of the universe cannot go. With the guide still in mid-disquisition, I decided silently to confront this challenge that life had seemed to orchestrate for me here, focusing my ruminations as reality does only on infrequent occasions.

I peered down the black corridor and, after an interval, whispered one word: "No!" "No" to oblivion; "no" to the black hole; "no" to death. In a flash, I believed in the eternity of all human souls in a way that all rote recitations of creeds had never nurtured in me. Like charitably parting company with Camille Flammarion about the significance of the size of galaxies, I now bid farewell philosophically to those who believed that "dust to dust" was all that could be said about the human story. I had an existential answer around which I would gather my life. This of course did not mean that there would not be times of doubt; far from it. In a fine essay, "Religion: Reality or Substitute?", C. S. Lewis says that believers sometimes look at all they are asked to affirm and are assailed with misgivings about the sheer improbability of it all; while skeptics and agnostics are discomforted at times by a reality which seems to shout that it is far more than it appears to be.

No, I would have to continue my journey in the semi-darkness where nothing is vouchsafed in stone; but after San Domitilla, what I can only call the "guts" of my consciousness had been converted. I would henceforth draw energy from the dead, in whose continued existence I somehow had no choice but to believe. I had been given something else as well: a mission, although it took a while for it to become apparent, since I was not religiously inclined at the time. I would pray for the dead—not an unusual practice in the Catholic tradition with its doctrine of the communion of saints. But my version of this kind of prayer was rooted in the experience of peering into the void and realizing that the names of the persons interred in the catacombs were lost to history. About them, I could do nothing; but I resolved that I would devote myself to remembering those who were "given" to me—that is, the deceased of my blood, friendship, work connections, and chance meetings—all in the corner of the space/time continuum in which I had been placed. My remembering would consist in "naming names"—to borrow a somewhat disreputable phrase—repeating them over time as if they were individual beads of an extended rosary.

People have sometimes taken me to task a bit for this practice, asking me why I don't pray more for the living. But of course, like many people, I do—for my living loved ones, for world peace, for those in poverty, to name a few concerns. However, there is no other explanation for why I devote the time to prayer for the dead other than that I feel impelled to do it. Others have laughed at my idea of "naming names"—as if God could forget people. Yet a similar argument could be advanced about the efficacy of all prayer. Christians pray for daily bread; does that mean God has to be reminded? No, God has asked us to pray for all sorts of things. As I see it from an earthly perspective, the naming of names in prayers for the dead maintains the deceased's membership in the human community—a holy mission for those who are summoned to do it.

For years, the future practice of this prayer vocation lay dormant within me. Two things were required to turn it from potency to action: equipment and a mechanism. For equipment, I needed some kind of place or thing upon which to record names—a solution to which problem offered itself by attending wakes, where a supply of remembrance cards with the deceased's name on it was available. In many cases I did not attend the wake, but a card was given to me nonetheless—a relative of a friend, a friend of a relative or work associate—once it was known that I was doing this as a spiritual practice. But what of my ancestors whose wakes I did not attend? What of my grade school teacher whose death I read about in the newspaper? For such as these I have blank saint's cards provided to me, in bulk if I were to need that many, by friendly religious sisters. I keep them in a small box in a filing cabinet and have come to regard them somewhat as unconsecrated hosts, eventually becoming "blessed" with the names of the dead persons.

Which brings me to the other piece of equipment, brought forth to address the dilemma of how to store the "consecrated" cards. A shoebox-like container like the one I used for the blank cards simply wouldn't do. A "tabernacle" enclosure of some sort was needed to house these holy names; and, happily, another object drawn—like the observer's chair—from the family reliquary fit the bill. When I was a boy, my mother showed me a small polished wooden box with a clear glass hinged lid in which she kept her small supply of jewelry. The occasion was a viewing of her latest multicolored earrings, which my father had given her at the then-exorbitant price—at least for a textile worker—of thirteen dollars. I remember admiring them but being more interested in the container, a fact of which my mother apparently took due note. Decades later in her retirement years, she asked me to retrieve something from her dresser. When I opened the drawer, there lay the box, and taped to the glass window was a three-word note in her own hand: "Give to Paul." The note is still attached, but now the box sits on the top of *my* dresser; and the contents are still jewels—only of another kind.

One thing remained: a mechanism or regimen for the prayer. Would I just remove a card at will, pray for the deceased, and then return it? No; what would be lost here would be the sense of being with the person over time. Taking the whole box in my hands and praying for all who were within, of course, was not an option, since the whole point of the exercise was the "naming of names." Finally, after due deliberation, I arrived at a rather pedestrian solution. Like many people, I enjoy reading; I customarily have two books going at the same time. The answer! I would use the cards as bookmarks, and then return them. For a while, I kept a card for an entire book; but being a slow reader and at the same time watching my collection grow, I quickly had to come up with a quantitative adjustment. The persons commended to my care would receive a portion of a book—one hundred pages, two hundred pages, depending on its length—and would be with me and I with them for a number of days (I rarely have time to sit and read for hours). Cathy, taking note of the modification of my original plan—whole books to fractions of books—once asked me how many pages she would get if the unthinkable happened and she pre-deceased me. I replied that she would get the entire *War and Peace* ... for starters!

There is nothing elaborate about the prayers I offer for the people given to me. When I open a book anew and find the card with the person's name where I previously stopped reading, I respond with a three- or fourfold intercession: (1) A thanksgiving to God for calling the person into being in the first place; (2) an expression of gratitude for the person's contribution to my life, if I am aware of it; (3) a plea that the person is now at rest or in joy or is journeying with hope thereto; and (4) a request that God will console those here on Earth who mourn the loss of the deceased. To me, the quality of the prayer is not what matters; it is the instances over and over again in which I name the name and, in some mysterious way, add whatever spiritual strength I have to that soul's passage to the divine precincts.

I have thus far resisted adding to the list the famous and notorious whose deaths are noted in all the media. I might offer a quick silent prayer, but I have confined my exercise of living with a name to those whom I have claimed have been "given" to me and are thus part of the community of the dead to which I have become, in some metaphysical sense, attached. However, in this circle of souls are those whose cards were passed on to me by friends or relatives. Thus it is that when I finally get to the person's name, I may have forgotten who they are—my only connection to them being that I am praying for them. I identify this kind of relationship as another way of "seeing" a soul by starlight.

I place cards of very recently deceased persons near, but not at, the top of the stack contained in the jewel box since, as I imagine it, others are "waiting." When I have finished being with the person, I return their card to the bottom of the stack, knowing that I will eventually return to them, if in God's providence, I live long enough. Residing at the bottom of the stack is a photograph: a wonderfully candid shot taken at an extended family party in the late forties. My mother stares into the camera with the somewhat fatigued look of one who has spent all day making sandwiches and preparing other refreshments; my father is behind her with a bit of a scowl or quizzical look—evidently he was not given time to pose. And I am there—a toddler hanging onto my mother's dress. For some reason, when I place a card back into the jewel box I commend that soul to my parents' care also, as if I could create across the frontier of death a new community of acquaintanceship that might not have been possible within the limits of terrestrial life.

To maintain community with the dead, especially in regard to the preservation of their names—that is how I would sum up my efforts in this area. Of course the names of most of the persons I am praying for are not really lost—like those of the ancient Romans—but are indeed recorded in a convenient location called a cemetery. What is lacking here, however, is the connectivity of the name with the human community, because a cemetery—at least under one view—is a ghetto for the dead, a concentration camp for remains, a venue one can avoid visiting and, therefore, ultimately a place of forgetting.

What I would prefer—that is, in the matter of the names contained in the confines of a cemetery—is clearly unworkable, and yet I cannot forbear mentioning it. Several years ago I ceased jogging due to hip and foot pain and took up bicycling as a replacement exercise. Biking in different townships locally, I would invariably come upon memorial squares of one kind or another located right within residential and even busy commercial neighborhoods. Most often they featured the names of, or were dedicated to, military heroes or other public benefactors—the name or names often being preserved on polished stone and surrounded by landscaping. The thing about them that pleased me was that the names were/are among us, occupying space—small, unobtrusive space where we live and work. Wouldn't it be wonderful, I have thought on many occasions, if the names of all the deceased could be so memorialized—every telephone pole, every sidewalk pane, every wall to be inscribed somewhere the moment a soul passes into eternity. Unlike cemeteries, these markers could not be missed, teaching us clearly that *we* are not with the dead but that the dead are with *us*. But, as I say, it is unfeasible; and so I will continue to work in my own way to keep the names of some of the deceased alive.

And others will work in their ways. I am thinking here of my niece Amanda, who created a momentary stir a few years ago just before she was to receive the sacrament of confirmation. Toward the end of her classes and in keeping with the tradition of the Catholic Church, she, like her confreres, was given the opportunity of picking a confirmation name, usually in honor of a saint or revered family member. Was it going to be Mary, Margaret, Catherine, or her mother's name, Theresa? Amanda chose Charles. Consternation! Was she goofing on the sacrament? Being a wiseacre? What would the bishop say? Those of us who got into immediate high dudgeon on the issue underestimated Amanda's native skills in theology. You see, she was born a twin—her womb-mate, a little boy who died at birth, was to be named Charles; Amanda had decided that

(VIII)

THE WEB OF FINALITIES

"In His city all things are made for each other."

C.S. Lewis, *Perelandra*

Www.com, the World Wide Web. "Are you online yet?" friends ask. The answer is still "No," although I don't know how long I can withstand a phenomenon that has taken reality by the throat and is gradually redefining the meaning of communicable space. But for now, I stare at the computer on my desk and think, "The greatest typewriter ever conceived." Anyone who has labored over term papers or otherwise made a living in part by writing can appreciate best, and be most grateful for, this mammoth advance over the old manual typewriter vouchsafed for us by computer technology.

But the Internet? That is a different story. I am told that using my computer solely for writing is missing 99 percent of its usefulness—a sentiment seconded by my bright young cousin, Jessica, who, hip deep in school assignments and projects, wonders aloud how anyone garnered information in the ages before the Web. I remember a class in American history in my undergraduate days way back in 1965, in which a prescient professor heralded the coming cybernetic revolution. Now that it is upon us, it has quickly established hegemony over culture, or at least popular culture, to the extent that it is almost as if one is not alive if not connected: "I surf, therefore I am." This is of course a negative spin, ignoring the alleged preponderant positives: a universe of data points now immediately accessible to the searcher in front of the screen. Yet I continue to temporize. Why? Fear of change, perhaps; an ingrained Luddite aversion to technological innovation, certainly; the much-remarked-upon annihilation of distance, oh yes. But there is more.

The Web is—what?—fifteen, twenty years old? And already there is a plethora of sociological studies about it, seen from every angle. We can expect to be inundated in the near and longer term. For every prognostication about the world becoming as one via its agency, there are now monographs highlighting its darker aspects. One that recently caught my attention contended that human boundaries will be rendered obsolete by internet usage and dependence, such that the isolated self, the celebrated individual—now slipping in and out of "Web roles"—will slowly disappear or, like the appendix, exist solely as an ornament attesting to a previous evolutionary phase.

A chilling forecast, but I do not share the sentiment. I see no signs of the attenuation of personal singularity in the initial Age of the Web; to the contrary, I see a marked expansion of it in recent years—not, to be sure, caused by the Web, but originating before the Web in the modern age, and now developing in parallel. And I am not talking about the individual as it has been mused about in philosophy or celebrated in lore—not rugged individualism, not individual rights, not Gary Cooper in *High Noon*. The specimen I have in view is a rather decadent, impoverished version of these: a particulate in motion, a careening metal sphere in a pinball world, unlubricated by the healing oils of commonality—manners and morals; customs and courtesies—now gone brittle.

The species can be viewed just about everywhere nowadays. Recently a pre-teen in our area wore his pajamas to school and caused a ruckus. During an interview, his mother said at one point that her son was "expressing his individuality." Or, there is the epidemic of boom boxes and car stereos, played with volume to the max, precisely to demolish others' limited spatial and aural sovereignty. A visual equivalent of this invasion are the many variations of the contemporary t-shirt. When I was a boy, t-shirts were fairly nondescript and worn only at work—that is, factory or construction type labor—or in recreative situations. Today they are ubiquitous, even at church liturgies, and are ablaze with messages—often "in your face"; sometimes violent or obscene; always, it seems, provocative. One grows weary of this constant affront and, in some seasons of desperation, looks longingly at the Amish, whose insistence on plain dress now seems to be born of wisdom.

But the contemporary weapon of choice in the struggle for individual self-aggrandizement is, for my money, the automobile. Full disclosure: our family has two, so my anti-car sentiments can quickly be dismissed as hypocrisy; though I would counter-argue that one has little choice but to own an auto short of living in a large metro area or, alternatively, giving up on mass society altogether and retreating to some kind of communal or monastic living arrangement. Moreover, bracketing off pollution, I have no argument with the car seen as the to-date most efficient means of conveyance from Point A to Point B. It is the car as an extension of the ego, the auto marketed as, and developed for, the purpose of making a statement or diminishing the self-worth of others that I have trouble with.

If one starts with the premise that all human beings are somewhere between marginally and fatally flawed, then putting at their disposal several tons of steel and encouraging them to use it for, among other things, attracting sex partners or winning a battle of wills brings predictably deleterious results. This can perhaps be most clearly seen in the ordeal known as the daily urban expressway commute, where drivers in their grim-faced separateness—a living rebuke to the adage "no man is an island"—attempt to best the competition in the game of lane-change chess. The inevitable collisions and pile-ups are becoming an increasingly apt metaphor for contemporary society, itself gradually devolving into a mere collection of atomistic individuals.

About the fractionalization of the human community—evident in so much of modern life—the Web, I believe, has not yet been shown to be an effective counterforce. For all its mind-expanding possibilities, for all the chat room connections it midwifes—some good, some not so good, all disembodied—it is also increasingly becoming like wallpaper in the lives of people—just there!—or, better perhaps, like a power saw in the corner of the basement, waiting to be fired up. This is not to say that the hope that the Web might promote peace among peoples is not a laudable sentiment. It just is misplaced in my view; for there is a another Web, engraved in the nature of things for this very purpose, that human beings are invited to discover, strand by strand, but which, regrettably, they too seldom search out.

My first inkling of this vast network (Pardon the pun about to be made!) emerged, I fully admit, from a previous technological innovation: television. In the late 1950s and early '60s, Leonard Bernstein and the New York Philharmonic presented a series of educational concerts on CBS—on Sundays, for adults; on Saturdays, for young people. I watched both. I distinctly remember one edition of the former where Bernstein, in order to demonstrate the conductor's art, showed how the opening measures of Beethoven's *Eroica* Symphony could vary considerably in receptive impression according to interpretations from Bruno Walter to George Szell. But it is the young people's concerts that are etched in my memory. The opening sequence showed the high school students arriving at the concert hall and going through the turnstiles—all smiles, sweaters and penny loafers. Sometimes I find myself imagining such a concert being held today—forty years later—with the teens, now with baggy jeans and nose rings, coming through the same entrance. Would a resurrected Bernstein—ever the music evangelist *cum* bridge-building diplomatist—try to show them how rap music was anticipated in the early nineteenth century German *lieder*?

In any case, in one edition of the series, Mr. Bernstein featured as a soloist on keyboard for Bach's Concerto No. 1 in D Minor, one Glenn Gould. I think part of his motive in getting Gould for the program was to expose the youngsters to someone who cared more for his art than for the approval of his peers—a sentiment hard for teens to share, but good for them to see. For as Gould performed the keyboard portion of the concerto, it was clear that he was in utter ecstasy; making love, as it were, to the music. It seemed that he was about to levitate from his seat, so exaggerated were his head gestures; and one could perceive the barely audible humming with the music—a Gould trademark, annoying to purists but endearing to his many devotees. I felt instantly drawn to this quirky, "weird" (as young people might term him) figure and sensed something else—a notion hard to put into words: I almost believed for a moment that his performance was given … for … me. That thought quickly dissipated in the onward rush of life activities, along with concern for Gould himself; though in my adult years I succumbed to Gouldmania: reading his biography; viewing the splendid film *Thirty Two Short Films about Glenn Gould*; and collecting his CDs of Bach keyboard music, humming and all.

Over the years as my music appreciation grew, I developed an affinity for certain composers—at one point, Edvard Grieg—and particular pieces of others, the *Hebrides Overture* of Mendelssohn being a favorite. Due to the highly idiosyncratic nature of this journey, there was always the sense—inchoate, of course; for if ever it was brought to mind it would be clearly seen to be preposterous—that somehow the music was for me and perhaps I for the music. There was nothing as startling as the Gould episode, though.

Then it happened again. In my twenties I gravitated to the music of Aaron Copland. I was attracted above all to the sense of landscape and atmosphere one receives in his musical descriptions of places, above all American locales. Once, while listening to the penultimate measures of the ballet suite *Appalachian Spring*, I was convinced again that I was somehow created to hear this music, and that Copland had been created to compose it … for me. Traditional mysticism might term such an apperception the achievement, or at least the beginning of an achievement, of oneness with Being; and although I am not adverse to such a description, I prefer one that preserves the idea of separateness in complementarity, as in partners executing a dance.

I am grateful to Copland, not only for the joy his music has given me, but for how his example started me on the investigation of a variety of music that I might have dismissed or overlooked. I am speaking of scores written for cinema. Copland, who must be regarded as one of the godfathers of this art form, wrote some memorable ones himself, including music for *Of Mice and Men* and *Our Town*. And I have sampled the output of his many progeny, from Franz Waxman and Jerome Moross to Miklos Rozsa, Elmer Bernstein, Maurice Jarre, and Jerry Goldsmith, down to such current practitioners as Randy Newman, Randy Edelman, and—a special favorite—James Horner. Another contemporary composer to whose work I am attracted is Thomas Newman, who wrote the scores for *Scent of a Woman*, *The Shawshank Redemption*, and *The Horse Whisperer*. Listening to certain of the piano passages from these movies, I get again the sense of creative linkage that has continued to haunt my consciousness. So great is my appetite for certain of this music that I have sometimes astonished Cathy by wanting to see a film or buy a video primarily to hear the score.

Two things this set of experiences has taught me. One is that for me—and countless others ("Music hath charms …")—music is a principle locus of mystical experience. The other is that, despite the *prima facie* irrationality of regarding these works as having been written for me, they are clearly not for everyone, or at least not for everyone in the sense of which I am speaking. Certain pieces or even short passages that plunge me into extended gooseflesh, I find, do not so affect others, who often prefer different selections that have little impact on me.

Here, then, was a phenomenon that invited exploration. I began with a consideration of the term that names my experience: teleology, the study of purposefulness as a pervasive aspect of the Real. The idea that Being was somehow rationally ordered was a notion taken for granted by many of our ancestors of ancient days and given a philosophical underpinning most notably by Aristotle. His doctrine of the four causal determinants of any existent—material, formal, efficient (propelling), and telic (final cause)—was one of the high points of Greek thought. I remember a professor in my college introductory philosophy course attempting in simplified form to explain it to a less-than-enthusiastic class. He gestured toward the podium behind which he had been standing a moment before, then advanced toward it and massaged the wood: "Material cause." Then he asked the class to imagine a blueprint or draftsman's drawing of what was to become the finished product: "Formal cause." Out of a reluctant male freshman made to stand up and perform a carpenter's sawing and hammering actions in pantomime, the prof instantly fabricated the efficient cause; and returning to the podium to continue his lecture, he demonstrated the final cause—the purpose for which the wooden structure was made. Purpose, final cause, finality—the ultimate cause/source of things.

But, " ... was made ... " —the passive voice. What if we wanted to describe final causation using the active voice? This would require as the subject of the proposition a "maker" or "definer" who invested the process with purposefulness to create the entity. In the above example, perhaps the person who commissioned the carpenter and draftsman to fashion the lectern. But what of nature and the universe? Is there a Maker who has brought forth all things and made of them a vehicle for his purposes? As the indispensable Father Copleston tells us (*A History of Philosophy*, Vol. I, Part 2), there is little evidence that Aristotle saw the concept of final cause as requiring a divine Finalizer. One who had no hesitation in making such a leap, however, was the mediaeval legatee of Aristotle, St. Thomas Aquinas, who included as one of his five proofs of the existence of God the argument from final causes, sometimes labeled the argument from design. Things in nature that lack knowledge, so the argument runs, nevertheless seem to act for a purpose, nearly always achieving a good result—say, in the case of flowers, which by attracting bees with their scent and nectar "force" the bees to be co-agents of pollination. But flowers cannot reasonably be deemed to have the foresight to plan such a convenient operation, hence the need to posit a Purposer or Designer who has instituted this mutually advantageous nexus whom, as St. Thomas says, everyone calls God.

Thus it was that Aristotle and Aquinas, each with differing refinements, gave philosophical flesh and bones to a widely shared perception of cosmic and terrestrial purpose. But the lifework of St. Thomas was barely completed when a process was underway in Western thought to denude Being of the transparent intelligibility everyone had heretofore assumed it had. From William of Ockham through Descartes and Hume to Immanuel Kant and beyond, philosophy began to regard such concepts as causation, order, and purpose as residing within the human mind and, in one way or another imposed, for the sake of convenience, on a reality in large part ultimately unknowable.

About midway through this history there occurred the Scientific Revolution —a wholly new mode of thinking, vindicated by rapidly arriving technological applications, that appropriated to itself the investigative field previously superintended by natural philosophy while, through the agency of the scientific method, deliberately excluded considerations of purpose. A classic case is evolution, the well-attested theory of the natural history of life that observes and records the success of species according to the development of advantageous mutations. Thus, St. Thomas might comment, say, on the camouflage of an insect, that it was "given" for the purpose of escaping predation; while science would merely say that it was a randomly emerging attribute that, since it worked well, enabled those who possessed it to survive but those lacking it to quickly perish, with fewer opportunities to reproduce. No "invisible hand" in natural history; no Mother Nature ensuring a balance; and, of course, no God.

Yet purpose-thinking dies hard. Even television nature shows, the scripts for which are presumably written by the scientifically literate, if not by scientists themselves, fall into it. Sometimes, for instance, in a presentation on herd animals when the subject is ritual or real combat among males for opportunities to mate, the commentator will observe of the victor of such jousts something on the order of "This way, he … " or even "This way, nature … *ensures* that the strongest genes will be passed on." As if there were intentionality located somewhere in the process, a concept that science must exclude. Or take this definition from a technical manual on household organic hazards I accidently perused: "Mold consists of microscopic organisms whose purpose in the ecosystem is to break down dead materials." This recidivism to purpose-thinking, even by the scientifically sophisticated, is not surprising, however. Philosophers of language have pointed out that the attempt to replace purpose discourse with one that uses merely functional expressions will create a language markedly different from general communication and extremely difficult to access. It seems that human beings (and here is the key!), when they are not thinking about it, resort to notions of purpose in their assessments of self and the world.

Still, the idea of finality and purpose is at best fighting a rear-guard action against the trend of all modern philosophy and science. Perhaps the greatest celebrator of its retreat was the 18th-century philosophe and social critic Voltaire. Voltaire, the cheerful skeptic; Voltaire, the enemy of metaphysical presumptuousness; Voltaire, the brooding sage who, deeply affected by the appalling loss of life in the Lisbon earthquake of 1755, turned henceforth in disgust from thinkers who perceived a highly articulated order in creation into which human pain and suffering were facilely dovetailed. Voltaire concentrated all of what he regarded as this looniness in the character of Dr. Pangloss in *Candide*—said to be a thinly veiled approximation of the philosopher Leibniz. In the Panglossian view there was an answer for all ambiguity and a subheading for all vagaries in the serene confidence that this was the best of all possible worlds; while for Voltaire, answers—whether to questions or longings—were in short supply. Said he: "We are equipped to calculate, weigh, measure, observe—all the rest is chimera."

I admire Voltaire. Though he spent a good deal of his career battling the church of which I am a member and questioning things that I hold dear, he is still my kin. In his refusal to accede to easy explanations of ultimate realities, he possesses the minimum qualifications to be a Dark Run mystic. And the peroration at the end of *Candide*, that the business of life was to "cultivate our gardens," is, in my estimation, the perfect advice to all who are "ascending the inclined plane." Still I must part company with him: he comes to bury Pangloss; I, to "shrink" him. With Voltaire I feel an ingrained resistance to such bald assertions, as that of Leibniz, that the world was a harmonious whole produced by God to serve divine ends; on the other hand, I cannot deny my experiences with Copland and Gould, Horner and Newman. What I am reduced to, in essence, and what I believe humanity is left with in the matter of the purposefulness of reality, is "strands" —strands at once of evidence and connectedness, strands like those of a spider's web. And such strands, as those who have studied arachnids will tell you, are thin but immensely strong.

A motion picture that raised my consciousness about these strands was *Amadeus*. The film tells the fictionalized story of

Mozart as seen from the perspective of rival composer Antonio Salieri. Mozart is a genius who writes down perfect compositions in finalized form that he hears in his head; Salieri plods, erases, revises, and with agony brings forth second-rate music—in his own self-regard, a mediocrity. Mozart comes to Vienna and makes a big splash, stealing the thunder and adulation from court composer Salieri. Salieri plots Mozart's demise and at the same time, in a parallel dramatic trajectory, wonders why God has visited such a fate upon him. In a climactic scene, he tricks a bedridden and unwell Mozart to finish the Requiem Mass in an all-night composing session. Salieri offers to help with secretarial services, but his true motives are to hasten Mozart's death and steal credit for the composition.

The stage is thus set for what I would submit is one of the most dramatic two-person scenes in all of cinema. At home, I ruined the videotape of the movie and disabled the replay button of the VCR, attempting to view it over and over again. The moviegoer observes Mozart hearing in his mind the parts of the *Confutatis* section of the Requiem—vocal and instrumental—and dictating them to a feverishly scribbling and about-to-be larcenous Salieri. Then the incalculable happens: Salieri, overwhelmed by the sublimity of the music and assisted by a divine self-forgetfulness, can contain himself no longer and utters: "This is wonderful!" Finality! The purpose for which both Mozart and Salieri were created—the convergence of artist and appreciator. It was as if, in another story, Adam and Eve had looked at the fruit of the tree and reflected that they had better things to do, or—more precisely—to see and hear, and left it uneaten. The moment, however, did not last, and Salieri went back to his plotting ways, ultimately being foiled.

Don't get me wrong: I am not saying that this Mozart/Salieri connection exhausted the purposes—if you accept the idea of purposefulness in the first place!—for which each was brought into being. The big picture is an immense cross-hatching of connectivities—hidden from us in part here below—with appreciators and receivers being every bit as important to the dance as creators and originators and where roles are constantly reversed and partners continually changed. That is why a dose of Voltairian skepticism relative to a comprehensive teleology is always in order. What we have been given, however, are moments on the level of "strands," when divine purpose can be glimpsed in beauty created and appreciated, truth uttered and understood, compassion offered and received. And always, when the connection is fully made, the poles disappear: there is no longer creator and receiver, but only the stuff of connectedness—the Being of beauty, truth, and love.

Another cinematic rendering of the strands of finality—similar in my mind to *Amadeus*, though few critics would likely associate the two motion pictures—is *It's a Wonderful Life*. The plot is familiar to almost everyone: George Bailey, played by Jimmy Stewart, is dissatisfied with his life as the president of a small-town building and loan. He dreams of the wider world, of college, of becoming an architect; but all his plans come to naught for one reason or another. Finally, when bank deposit money turns up missing—due to the carelessness of his uncle—he decides to commit suicide; there is nothing to live for anyway. An angel ends up showing George how life would have been different and the poorer if he had never existed. In the end, the missing money is supplied to Bailey by a host of friends who think the world of him; and George discovers how important a person he truly is.

It's a Wonderful Life placed nicely in the American Film Institute's top one hundred films of the twentieth century; and it has been lavishly praised by actors, directors, and other film craftsmen. But in a league with the Oscar-winning *Amadeus*? "I don't think so," I can almost hear these people saying. *Amadeus* is all angst, absurdity, and ultimate irresolution—perfectly in phase with trends in the arts since the beginning of the twentieth century; it therefore qualifies as being "serious." *It's a Wonderful Life*, on the other hand, has a happy ending, leaving audiences aglow; thus, while given due deference, it ultimately would be labeled a "sentimental favorite" or a "Christmas classic."

But it isn't true! The two movies tell the same story. George and Antonio are afflicted with a similar malady of soul: they are both chasing images and don't know who they really are. Bailey has to be shown; Salieri in the end doesn't care to find out. Admittedly, the "Panglossian index" in *It's A Wonderful Life* is high, as Clarence the angel almost measures the hole left in reality were George never to have existed. One can imaginatively glimpse Voltaire wincing in the last row of the theater. Still the point survives the exaggeration: our lives are much larger than we think and are enshrouded by a purposefulness we can only guess at. And for me, there is an added bit of fantasy that unites the two motion pictures. The dramatic context that surrounds all the action in *Amadeus* is Salieri's confession—that is, a sacramental confession—to a priest who, at the end of the movie, is so staggered by the narration of the events that he is unable to offer the penitent counsel or absolution. But, in my mind, there was one surefire penance to prescribe for Salieri—requiring, admittedly, a large suspension of disbelief: He would be instructed to watch *It's a Wonderful Life* and make the appropriate inferences. Perhaps he viewed it in purgatory as he passed through.

Mention of sacraments puts me in mind of my own religious tradition and its famous analogy for the purposefulness and connectivity that, it asserts, characterizes the Church: the allegory of the Body of Christ found in I Corinthians 12. Much of the epistle, and this passage especially, highlights St. Paul's effort to heal the factionalism and animosities that had overtaken the Corinthian church. The body was the perfect counter-image to the situation there: individual members would be analogized as parts or organs, underscoring the theme of complementarity in unity. With the emphasis on unity, the body parts imagery allowed St. Paul fertile ground for commentary on what ailed his addressees. Some organs or body components, so his analysis ran, seem more attractive, more essential, more worthy of esteem than others—say, the eye as compared to the foot. But this is not the case—all are necessary because the body is the reality in view and is not complete with the loss of any of them; hence all are worthy of honor. In the middle of this discourse Paul anchors his thematic to a straightforward teleology: "God has set each member of the body in the place He wanted it to be." Take that, Antonio Salieri!

It is well-known that those who craft arresting imagery such as this have one or, at most, two points to make, after grasping which, the reader must discard the metaphor. Students of the parables of Jesus are quite familiar with this. Take the parable of the wise and foolish virgins from the Gospel of St. Matthew. Ten bridesmaids go out to await the arrival of the groom: five carry additional oil for their torches; five do not. The groom delays his arrival far into the night, by which time all the torches are going out. When the groom is announced, the foolish bridesmaids have to make a dash to the market to buy more oil, while the wise have enough. When the foolish virgins return they find that the door to the bridal chamber is barred and they are not allowed in. The moral? Be ready at all times for the return of Christ; even if He delays, He is coming. It is entirely missing the point or, better, confusing the issue to wonder, as I once did, why the wise virgins did not share their oil with the foolish.

Similarly, the image of the Body of Christ teaches the dignity of all in their separateness and the unity that emerges from mutual esteem; but it is asking more of an allegory than it can deliver to try to extract, in this instance, the specific metaphorical contribution of, say, the pancreas. Yet, despite this commonsense caveat, I have found myself musing, when it comes to the body analogy, on what is going on in the capillaries. I guess I am trying to create my own allegory or extend, perhaps illegitimately, the old one in order to meditate on purposes and connections that are minute or that seem inconsequential. The thing about teleology as I have hitherto described it is that, however much it strained one's credulity, it was at least understandable on the level of complementarity: Thus Aaron Copland and I; Mozart and Salieri; George Bailey and his family and friends; and the separate parts of the Body of Christ. But as in most everything else in the Dark Run, things are not always that clear, and the bigger picture may be sometimes found in the smaller arenas. It is here, I believe, that we are invited to become explorers in what I now call the Capillaries of Being.

My first and best teacher in this discipline was my mother, Myrtle Vincent, who was, in her own self-description, "Judy Friendly." By this she referred to her proclivity to make connections with people even when the occasion didn't demand it, or even discouraged it. At a bus stop, she wouldn't just nod to others, she would attempt an icebreaker such as "They've been running late the last few days," or in the supermarket, noticing what another shopper had in his/her cart, she would venture, "That's a good price for bananas." On such fragile hooks she hung conversations that sometimes did not end until circumstances naturally brought a parting of the ways. Myrtle was notorious for talking with police officers, sanitation men, construction-site workers, and elevator operators. At home, she would excitedly relate in great detail the substance of these conversations, suggesting that she regarded having had them as something of an accomplishment.

Why did she do it? Myrtle, of course, was somewhat gregarious and always a little curious; some might even term her nosy. She was also compassionate, and liked to talk to people who had a hard job—thus, construction workers and the like. But I think the word "accomplishment" comes closest to the truth. Myrtle sensed, if she did not know, that she was somehow performing work that was critical and was even a task that God had given her to do, though she would never describe it that way. There was finality in it; but, unlike the body analogy, it wasn't altogether clear what the purpose was. For lovers of the spiritual Dark Run, this is precisely what makes it interesting, and why it is that I carry on my mother's work.

A co-worker related to me that written down somewhere in manuals for correct deportment in a business setting there are descriptions of so-called "idiot salutations"—for instance, overly enthusiastic greetings, especially to people one does not know, or saying hello several times to the same person. Such behavior is always to be avoided, lest one be thought an oddball; as everyone knows, oddballs don't get promoted.

I am the King of the Idiot Salutation. I make the effort in honor of my mother, but also because I am convinced that deep within every person there is a longing for their existence to be recognized. As long as there is this awe-striking possibility, and in the knowledge that there are finalities of which I know nothing but in which I am nevertheless asked to participate, I will say hello even to persons at work whom I have greeted already and to persons on the street whom I have never met.

The great enemy in the effort to establish fleeting connections with strangers out of doors is sunglasses (although a recent innovation, the cell phone, runs a close second). I should not say an unkind word against sunglasses, however; a terrible squinter, I avoided wearing them for years, but now have embraced them for aid on bright days. Still, eye protection is only part of their allure for many; sunglasses are, or have become, in addition, an essential component of the "coolness" package, along with the right clothes and the right line. Sporting shades, the aspirant to hipness is able to mask vulnerability, longing, incompleteness, joy, or enthusiasm until he sees which way the wind blows. Meanwhile, others who look his way as they pass by are reticent to speak since they see no encouragement in the black opaqueness that guards the door to the wearer's soul.

Anyone's life experience, I venture, will prove this theory. A few years ago, Cathy and I attended one of many baseball games at McCoy Stadium—home of the Pawtucket (R.I.) Red Sox, a minor-league affiliate of the Boston Red Sox. Arriving later than usual for an early evening game, we had to find seats in the first base/right field stands. The setting sun was directly in our eyes, so on came the sunglasses. Seated immediately next to Cathy was a young girl with her father one seat beyond. Several times I noticed her looking our way, but she said nothing. By the fourth inning, we were able to remove our glasses; shortly thereafter, I noticed Cathy and the little girl chatting between innings about the latter's doll collection.

Another connection made that might not have been—that is what struck me then about this incident and haunts me still. Here was the capillary action of the human story: hidden from view, unlike the larger organs of the "body," yet somehow integral, somehow necessary to its health and integrity. Or, using the original metaphor, here is another strand in a vast web that God, a benign and industrious spider, is co-creating along with the entire human race. It is this web, I would submit, rather than the Internet, that the human person should more fully explore; it is this web that is balm for all the aches of particularity that afflict the soul; and it is the contemplation of this web that helps us to hold in check our worst impulses. Though I have often admired those who are committed to non-violence, I have never been a pacifist; yet, with this web in view, the idea of wounding another human being in any way, much less killing him, reaches a new, perhaps life-changing, level of repugnance and unacceptability.

What is God, the Spider, ultimately making with the strands of Her own Being? As a lover of the Dark Run, I am happy to report that no one, in finality, knows. We are like Al Pacino as Frank Slade toward the end of *Scent of a Woman*, delicately fingering the face of Chris O'Donnell, whom he cannot see but has come to love. Yet, another image may bring us a step closer. The nineteenth chapter of the book of Revelation describes the Church about to be united with God at the end of time. She is conceived as a bride preparing to be married, and is adorned with an appropriately dazzling linen dress. The dress, the author tells us, is the virtuous deeds of the saints.

As always, I love to play a bit with the imagery I have gratefully received from my faith tradition. I see the bride as the human community, and the dress is, stitch by stitch, all the relationships in history that individuals have formed. There will, of course, be many patterns representing intimacy, kinship, and friendship; separate designs witnessing to the threads that have bound creators and receivers; and, not to be dismissed, the connections given birth by Judy Friendliness. There will also be huge rents in the garment, signaling the many horrible episodes of man's inhumanity to man, and smaller voids where opportunities to connect were missed or ignored.

My guess is that, in spite of the mixed picture, the divine Husband will regard the garment that clothes His beloved bride as genuinely lovely. This is not surprising: God is also its Seamstress and its living Threads. Even before she died, Myrtle Vincent, one of the innumerable co-seamstresses on the project, could have told you just how beautiful those threads are.

(IX)

THE STAR AT THE END OF THE RIVER

"That we do not know you is your perfection and our hope. The darkness keeps us near you."

Wendell Berry

Orion the hunter is easily one of the most recognizable star patterns in the heavens, perhaps nosed out slightly in popular familiarity and cultural usage by the asterism known as the Big Dipper. After all, the Dipper—in addition to having made its way onto the Alaskan flag, into paintings by Van Gogh, and into numberless literary allusions—contains the so-called "pointer stars," used for centuries by seamen and other nighttime observers to locate that indispensable stellar navigational aid known as the North Star. Still, what Orion lacks in critical celestial placement, it more than makes up for in sheer brilliance and superior verisimilitude.

For starters, the constellation features an eye-catching three-star chain, which, once the whole assemblage has been accounted for, is instantly seen to be the waist or belt of a man. Below and angled downward is another, dimmer string of three stars constituting a semi-realistic sword. Together, the belt and sword, if they were not otherwise metaphorically deployed, make a more compact and much brighter "little dipper" than the asterism that bears that nickname. The head of the champion is marked by a tight triangle of lesser stars, which, while not exactly looking like a cranium, is at least a convenient placeholder for one and, in that capacity, superior to what many star groupings are supposed to pass for in the way of representation. For shoulders and feet (or knees, as some fanciful images have it), four stars surround the belt and sword at clear points of an irregular quadrangle. Two are typical near bright stars; the other two—right shoulder and left foot/knee—constitute Orion's principal claim to naked-eye glory. Only a limited number of constellations have a star of the first magnitude of brightness—the Big Dipper and its parent constellation, Ursa Major, have none. It is rare indeed to find a constellation, like Orion, with two in this category, indeed two of the fifteen brightest stars in the sky.

Marking the left shoulder is the delightfully orange-red star Betelguese—an odd-sounding name that is derived from an Arabic word meaning "armpit." Termed by astronomers a super-giant, it is so large in diameter that, were it to be placed in the position of the sun, the earth would be inside it; yet for all that, it is of extremely tenuous density. At the left foot of Orion is the brilliant white Rigel—one of the brightest stars in the galaxy, dimmed only by its extreme distance, and boasting cinematic fame as one of the names of Ben-Hur's chariot horses.

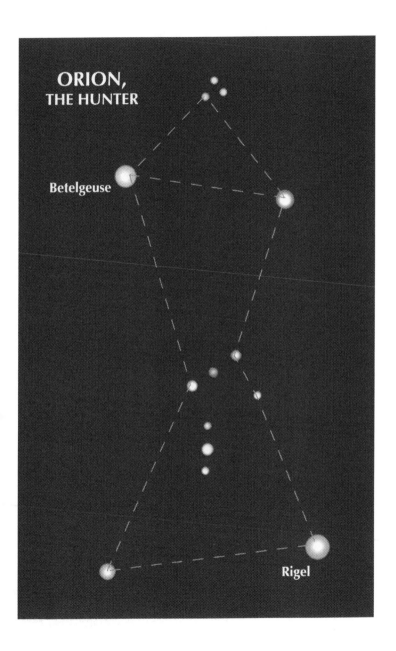

Sometimes when gazing at Orion and not disposed to see the constellation as a human being, I visualize the quadrangle stars as the corners of a jewel box surrounding black velvet, on which is displayed small diamonds (belt and sword). And, lest I forget, there is one more treasure in the constellation, slightly hidden from view but, once glimpsed, exceeding any diamond in beauty. I am speaking of the middle star in the sword—Tennyson's "single misty star"—which is actually a nebula, M-42 in M. Messier's catalogue. Even binoculars and the smallest telescopes reveal a vast cloud of glowing gas with tendrils and filaments surrounding other stars not visible to the unaided eyes. Actually a star nursery over thirteen hundred light years distant, the Orion Nebula has ravished observers since the beginning of optics and would certainly make the list of the top five showpieces of the heavens.

Like the Dark Run itself, Orion has its several seasons, which veteran observers celebrate. To me, nothing can surpass the rising of Orion on a late evening in October—its great bulk clearing the horizon like a hero arriving to save the day. I like less the melancholy Orion of spring—late March to late April—when the constellation appears in the west after sunset like a slowly declining athlete at the end of his career. But most devotees would probably say that Orion's greatest appeal is in winter, when it stands upright, bisected by the meridian and reigning over the night from the high south.

I will get a chance to see that later tonight under optimum conditions but just now, in the early evening, I am looking at Orion, what of it I can see, from the back deck of my home, my own observing station. The great hunter is about halfway up the vault of the southeastern sky on a night of excellent transparency in this, the Dark Run at the end of January: the "dead of winter," as some would have it; but I prefer to call it the "womb of the year," mindful that so much of earthly life is held in abeyance between potency and act, awaiting the summons of the equinoctial sun a month and a half hence. In any case, I am traveling to Frosty Drew for a night of mid-winter observing, albeit without any fellow pilgrims except my brother-in law Norm, who will meet me there.

Cathy and I have a quick supper of soup and sandwich while she tries to decide whether to visit her sister or stay at home to get further into a novel she has just started, there being no question of her accompanying me on a night of below-freezing and descending temperatures. As I kiss her good-bye after loading up the car, she still has not made up her mind about what to do, and is preparing to call her sister.

My departure is expeditious, since I am not bringing the usual complement of equipment—only hand-held 50 mm binoculars, which I will wear around my neck, a star chart I have drawn in pen and ink, and my flashlight. I have brought a couple of tapes to listen to on the way down, but I don't use them, preferring instead to think about the evening's activities ahead. My purpose in traveling to Frosty Drew on a night of such contra-indicative temperatures is to see the celestial treasures of a winter night under dark sky conditions—a rare experience indeed, since most of my journeys here occur in more benign seasons. I have another goal also—one that I have told no one about, but which nevertheless is close to my heart.

On arrival, I am surprised to see a couple of extra cars besides Art's, Dave's, and Norm's, who has beaten me here again. I quickly strap on my binoculars, secure my heaviest winter coat, and momentarily consider whether to achieve my secret aim right now; but, deciding against it (Norm might begin to worry about me), I leave the chart and flashlight in the car for later. Walking around to the entrance to the observatory, I veer off the walkway before entering, and stroll out onto the adjoining field: scene of so many enjoyable observing sessions under more bearable conditions, but now empty. The ground is snowless and hard underfoot; the wind has diminished. I can almost sense the cold gathering. Aloft, Orion is nearing culmination; the moment of prime opportunity for accomplishing my mission is quickly approaching, but I must first put in an appearance inside the observatory. From within, I can hear several disembodied voices in the eerie way they project outside the dome through the telescope's observing gap.

Inside I see Norm talking to Art, while Dave is speaking to a gentlemen at the eyepiece. Two more young men are behind him, waiting to look. In the wall curve to the left are a brave family of three—father, mother, and a ten- or eleven-year-old daughter—huddled against the cold, perhaps having second thoughts about the evening's choice of activities. I smile at them as Norm sees me for the first time. Greeting each other warmly, I grouse, "Beat me down here again!" "That's because I live closer!" Norm laughingly responds. I say hello to Art and exchange pleasantries.

"What are we looking at?" I ask, but do not wait for the answer. It is obvious from the southward azimuth of the telescope and its angle of ascent that it is pointed at the Orion Nebula. I immediately get in line for a view, my turn coming in less than a minute, it seems. As I peer in, I emit a slight gasp: an awe-striking object in almost any instrument, the beauty of M-42 grows without relative diminishment with every increase in optical aperture. In the observatory's telescope, the greenish color of the gaseous clouds is more clearly marked than I have noted before, and the stars within are much more easily seen. I linger for long seconds at the eyepiece, then surrender my place, noting that the family has lined up for a second look—the only sensible thing to do. I queue up behind them with a smile of satisfaction: I have already accomplished the secondary purpose of coming down this evening.

I chat with Norm and Dave after my second look, while Art and some of the others are taking theirs. When it is over, a curious tentativeness overtakes everyone. Clearly, it is time to view another object, yet it does not seem to be forthcoming. As I watch the family's young child shiver against the cold, I sense a providential gap that will enable me to get to my main business here tonight. Casually, I venture to Dave: "What about taking a look at M-81 and M-82?" He quickly agrees: two galaxies in the same field make for a dazzling sight; and they are in Ursa Major, which is now relatively high in its northeast winter station, well-placed for viewing. I have seen these objects many times in small telescopes and even in binoculars—two faint fuzzy patches between six and nine million light years distant! One has its face inclined to the line of sight, the other is seen more nearly edge-on, appearing something like a narrow cigar. I have strained to view these differences in the small instruments I have used, perceiving them only (if I am honest) because I

The Orion Nebula

saw photos of the galaxies before the viewing session. But the observatory's telescope, with even moderate magnification, should show the contrasts easily.

I won't find out tonight, however. For some reason, after making the suggestion of a viewing object, I have conveniently fallen out of the conversation: Norm is still talking to Dave, Art is conversing with the family, and the other gentlemen are at the table consulting a star map. Now, while everyone is preoccupied and the creaking music of the observatory dome sounds a near 180-degree turn, is my chance to escape. I slowly but deliberately slip out the door and trot to the car for my map and flashlight. As I make my way back to the observing field, I can hear again the voices inside the observatory, now oriented to the northeast; I, on the other hand, will be looking south, not a normally mystical direction for me; that is, until recently.

I look up again at the mighty hunter Orion, standing nearly upright in the high south and compelling obeisance from all nighttime observers. The curious thing is, however, that if he would allow you to un-transfix your gaze for a moment, there are any number of other notable stellar aspirants for attention in the immediate vicinity. To the upper right of Orion (as seen from the Earth) is the constellation Taurus (the Bull), whose eye is the bright orange-hued star Aldabaran, and on whose shoulder is the familiar and charming Pleiades. To the upper left is another constellation—Gemini—which boasts two first-magnitude stars, Castor and Pollux. More horizontally to the left is the constellation Canis Minor, the lesser companion dog of Orion, with its gleaming white star Procyon. And to the lower left shines the shimmering blue-white Sirius, the brightest star in the sky, situated in the heart of Canis Major, the greater dog. Even under Orion's feet, a small stellar assemblage sometimes attracts a look: it has no bright star, but after patient scrutiny can be seen to resemble the crouching hare, Lepus.

Streaming outward from Orion as center, there is only one direction that does not at first invite attention. Immediately to the right (west) and down from the Hunter lies a sparse and unbright scattering of stars signifying, at first glance, almost nothing. Year after year, as I have looked for the autumnal advent of Orion with joy and hope, and later enjoyed his presence and that of his gleaming companion constellations all winter, I have passed over this section of sky without thought of tarrying. But now, fully embracing the concept that finding the object of desire requires, more often than not, an averting of one's gaze to initially unpromising locales, and sensing that I am about to participate in the dance of a personal finality—or at least one only shared by lovers of the Dark Run—I will tonight keep watch on this section of sky.

For here is Eridanus, The River—a rambling constellation, associated in lore with the Nile and the Euphrates and other, mythical, streams—a stellar assemblage made, if ever there was one, for mediocre mystics. One almost has to strain to make out the stars; yet among them, veiled from view, is one whose very hiddenness has become a summation metaphor for all my hopes and my strivings. That is why what I propose to do—trace out the constellation using my map—is as much a personal prayer as an astronomical exercise, and why I wanted to be alone.

I begin in close proximity to Orion, at the headwaters of the great river, where resides the star Curza—an Arabic word meaning "footstool" (i.e., Orion's). For the ancients, stars in the immediate vicinity, it seems, were drafted into the Orion story in one way or another—a further testament to his dominance. In more recent times, professional astronomers, while recognizing that the constellations bequeathed to us by our ancestors were still a useful method of dividing up the night sky, nevertheless needed to codify their boundaries. In this process, Curza, though in close proximity to Rigel, was officially designated to be in Eridanus. Along the way, it got a new name too: Beta Eridani. Beta Eridani? Astronomers decided that not only were traditional constellations effective sky locaters, but they could also be pressed into service to designate stars in a more systematized fashion than the fanciful names associated with the myths of antiquity. Thus, the genitive case of the mostly Latin names of the constellations is paired with a Greek letter beginning with Alpha, usually for the brightest star in the group, and descending in magnitude through the entire alphabet (Beta Eridani therefore means "the second-brightest star of Eridanus"; Gamma would be the third; and so on). When astronomers run out of Greek letters they use letters from the customary alphabet, or numbers.

Before beginning my slow journey star by star, I try to get a sense of the whole constellation by visually sweeping. The ancients divided the River into upper and lower streams: upper, from Curza to Pi Ceti (A star the River shares with the constellation Cetus, the Whale); lower, from Pi Ceti to … well, I can't bring myself to mouth the word just yet. In any case, the entire structure of the constellation describes an ever-southward movement, but in gradual increments, due

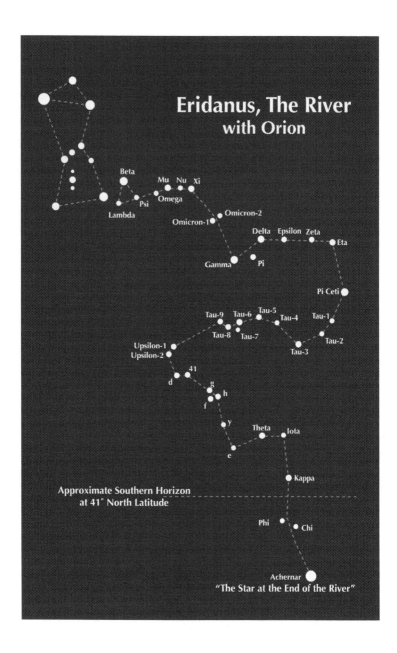

Eridanus, The River
with Orion

Beta

Mu Nu Xi

Omega

Psi

Lambda

Omicron-1 Omicron-2

Delta Epsilon Zeta

Eta

Gamma Pi

Pi Ceti

Tau-9 Tau-6 Tau-5

Tau-4 Tau-1

Tau-8 Tau-7

Tau-3 Tau-2

Upsilon-1
Upsilon-2

41

d

g

f h

y

Theta Iota

e

Kappa

Approximate Southern Horizon
at 41° North Latitude

Phi Chi

Achernar
"The Star at the End of the River"

to westward, then eastward thrusts. Indeed, the first flow is to the west.

Time to begin. Sharing the "headwaters" position in a compact triangle with Beta are the less-bright stars Psi and Lambda. From here the river journey begins in a western vector from Beta to Omega only a few degrees away. Then the River displays the first of four "false norths"—that is, it takes a short northwest turn from Psi to Mu Eridani, after which it briefly levels out again in a westward flow to Nu and Xi. From this point begins the first of six "southern drops," which characterize the true and final direction of this the Mother of Celestial Waters. From Xi through two stars, both designated Omicron, to the bright star Gamma, the River traces a southwesterly plunge of about twelve degrees. From this point begins the second short "false north" through Pi to Delta. Then it is western sailing again through Epsilon and Zeta to Eta. Now begins the second southern turn, but a gradual, southwesterly one of five degrees or so to Pi Ceti.

I stop for a moment to review, since I have finished the so-called "upper stream," although it is less than a third of the way to the River's end. I am glad, because I have been able to pick out all the chief stars in this stream from Curza to Pi Ceti. Looking back at my progress thus far, I see that the "upper stream" appears as two irregular half-circles or wings, with Gamma as a mid-point.

Now to press on. From Pi Ceti the River flows due south, or nearly so, for over ten degrees of celestial latitude (called "declination")—the third of the six "drops." Here we are among nine stars, all designated Tau Eridani. Between Tau-2 and Tau-3, the river brakes its southern dive and executes a switchback to an almost easterly direction—a phenomenon that prompted the ancients to name Tau-2 Argentenar, or "bend of the river." Though we are traveling eastward, we are indeed far south of our starting point. Between Tau-8 and Tau-9 there is another very brief "false north" before the river executes a large eleven-degree "southern drop," but still in a generalized eastern direction, to Upsilon-1 and 2, also named Beemim and Theemim. I find myself gently whispering these strange-sounding Semitic names as if urging on the stars, conceived of as the flow of a river, to complete their journey to its end.

As if in response, Eridanus turns on a dime to the southwest and drops nearly twenty degrees of declination, its flow represented by a number of run-of-the-mill stars designated by numbers and non-Greek letters. I am not there yet, but I am acutely aware that my journey is now inexorably approaching the tree line—something I just hadn't factored into my preparations, as if a thick atmosphere near the horizon wasn't enough! Well, I have come this far; the only thing to do is proceed.

Moving southwesterly from Theemim, I can see stars "d" and "41" only five degrees down, and then west southwesterly, and yes, I pick out a small triangle of stars designated "f," "g," and "h." Now a short distance south, perhaps three degrees, and there is the dim star "y." I can barely see it, and I'm not sure if I have positively identified it. The star "e," still farther south, I realize now, will definitely be beyond my vision. But no matter—at least temporarily—because the River now makes the last of its "false norths" to the fairly bright star

Theta, and I rejoice because I can clearly see it even within the thickening horizon; it is a night of such excellent transparency. Immediately to its west is the less-bright star Iota, which I strain to make out and tell myself that I have. Now the River, my map tells me, flows south for good—next stops being "s" and Kappa. I try hard to see them, but it is no use; I have reached the end of the celestial line, but the River has not. Its destination, its consummation, is just south, beyond my ability to see.

I hang my head in a half-serious moment of disappointment. Kappa, if I could see it, is just above the absolute limiting southern horizon for this latitude: forty-one degrees north. Just a few stars, and degrees, south shines the luminous end-point of the river, a finality I knew before I came here tonight I would not be able to view. In a sense, I set up this whole exercise in order to come to a mild grief; I traced the whole River to ritualize my own poverty of spirit. What I am bereft of is Achernar—Arabic for "End of the River." Achernar— the name the ancients gave to "The Star at the End of the River"—the last and brightest star in Eridanus; indeed, the only bright star in the constellation, and one of the brightest stars in the sky.

I know my spiritual mission here tonight has been a success, because I am suddenly overcome with the urge to get in the car, drive out of the observatory grounds, and speed south down Route 1 until Achernar comes into view—perhaps to the legendary Key West which, at about twenty-four degrees north latitude, would reveal the star of my desire at least a few degrees above the horizon. Yet, though this would satisfy my curiosity, it would not be balm for my longing; for, to me, Achernar is much more than a star, Eridanus more than a river. They have instead become a grand personal metaphor—the matter given by God (stars, sky), the form contributed by human imagination (the image of a river). No, not personal; this is a metaphor for all mediocre mystics and ascenders of the inclined plane; for those who are comfortable in ordinary time; and for those who discover mystery, not by staring into the brilliance of Orion, but by averting their gaze into less-promising fields close by.

Eridanus is the human un-drama of those who live the unheralded life. A dim constellation, prey to meanderings, switchbacks, and temporary false directions, the River is the confusing jumble that is the best we can, at times, make of our lives: we, that is, who, unlike the stars of Orion, but like the stars of Eridanus, are relatively unknown and perhaps far from incandescent. Yet for all our mistakes and struggles, the flow of our lives is unidirectional, if only incrementally so. We are headed for a bright consummation—the divine presence itself, of which Achernar, in all its luminous glory yet temporarily hidden from view, is a particularly apt metaphor.

Is that hiddenness a tragedy, or at least a pity? No! My joy in the monthly return of the Dark Run has taught me otherwise, at a level deeper than "explanations"; and my experience tonight, I suddenly realize, has put a fresh nuance into my conviction. The thing that prevents me from seeing Achernar is the ground upon which I am standing: forty-one degrees north latitude, my home! This is where I live; this is my history, the "lot marked out for me." This is where my ancestors labored; where

I have made precious bonds of kinship, friendship, and love; where I have tramped fields and woodlands that are now part of my very being.

I thought of this exercise as a prayer; and truly it was: the kind that Eridanus and the hidden Achernar, like the Dark Run itself, invite the children of space/time to make. A prayer of patient waiting for the yet-to-be-revealed and, at the same time, of joyful gratitude for the present moment. There is only one thing to say in response: a softly whispered "Amen."

"Paulie! They've got M-1 in the telescope at high power. You've got to see it!" It's Norm who has startled me out of my reverie; he must have finally noticed me missing and decided to retrieve me. I turn to hear more, expecting him to ask me what specifically I'm doing; but he immediately falls silent, entranced by the winter splendor above. How long have I been out here? Apparently I not only lost track of time but failed to hear the observatory dome move on to a new object. M-1!—number one in M. Messier's list, also known as the Crab Nebula—is the remnant of an exploding star, whose filaments suggest the shape of the many-legged crustacean who gave it its nickname. Located in Taurus, it was likely first noted by Chinese astronomers in the year AD 1054, who designated it a "guest star" in the constellation. The nebula has a very low surface brightness, making it a difficult observing challenge for those, like me, who own small instruments and who must habitually observe in suburbia.

Suddenly, I'm completely back, and glad to be. Yes, I really want to see M-1. Just to view it will immediately unite me with

The Crab Nebula

those who scanned the sky a millennium ago and with many tonight across the Earth who have it on their observing list, as they, along with me and thousands of others, keep night watch during the Dark Run. It also now comes to me that "home" has a thousand faces in which I find delight: it is Norm standing next to me, it is Cathy curled up with a book and ready to turn off the light, it is grocery shopping tomorrow. Turning away from the south and its (for the moment) unattainable prize, I say to Norm: "Let's get in there and look at that nebula."

But, as we walk to the observatory door, I can't help but take one more backward glance. Beyond that southern horizon, at the end of that river, lies the source of all beatitude, the gathering point of all finalities. In times to come, I and all my brothers and sisters of the earth will bathe in the healing, unifying rays of Achernar; yet we will somehow also retain the individual joys that have animated our earthly lives— even night darkness. The unfinished business and pleasures of tomorrow, of the rest of my life, await me; but now that veiled destination—my heart's desire—will never be far from my mind. I will see you there!

BIBLIOGRAPHY

Abbott, Walter J., S.J. *The Documents of Vatican II*. Baltimore: The America Press, 1966.

Allen, Richard Hinckley. *Star Names: Their Lore and Meaning*. New York: Dover Publications, 1963.

Baba Ram Dass. *Be Here Now*. New York: Crown Publishing Group, 1971.

Bachelard, Gaston. *The Poetics of Space*. Boston: Beacon Press, 1969.

Baum, L. Frank. *The Wonderful Wizard of Oz*. New York: William Morrow and Co., 1987.

Berry, Wendell. *The Collected Poems of Wendell Berry*. San Francisco: North Point Press, 1987.

_____. *Life is a Miracle: An Essay Against Modern Superstition*. New York: Perseus Books Group, 2000.

Bolt, Robert. *A Man for All Seasons.* New York: Vantage Books, 1990.

Bradbury, Ray. *The Golden Apples of the Sun.* New York: Doubleday and Co., Inc., 1953.

Brown, Raymond, E., S.S.; Fitzmyer, Joseph A., S.J.; and Murphy, Roland E., O. Carm., eds. *The Jerome Biblical Commentary.* Englewood Cliffs, N.J.: Prentice-Hall, Inc., 1968.

Burckhardt, Jacob. *The Civilization of the Renaissance in Italy.* New York: Harper and Row, 1958.

Burnham, Robert, Jr. *Burnham's Celestial Handbook: An Observer's Guide to the Universe beyond the Solar System.* New York: Dover Publications, Inc., 1966.

Campbell, Joseph. *The Power of Myth.* New York: Doubleday, 1988.

Chesterton, G.K. *Orthodoxy.* New York: Dodd, Mead and Co., 1908.

Christian Prayer: The Liturgy of the Hours. New York: Catholic Book Publishing Co., 1970.

Conant, Ruth Sanger. *Jesus Christ, the Liberator.* Brooklyn, N.Y.: Pageant-Poseidon, Ltd., 1971.

Copleston, Frederick, S.J. *A History of Philosophy, Vol. I, Part II.* Garden City, N.Y.: Doubleday and Co., 1962.

Cross, F. L., ed. *The Oxford Dictionary of the Christian Church.* London: Oxford University Press, 1974.

Dawkins, Richard. *The God Delusion.* London, Bantam Books, 2006.

Day-Lewis, Cecil. *The Aeneid of Virgil.* Garden City, N.Y.: Doubleday Anchor Books, 1953.

Edwards, Paul, ed. *The Encyclopedia of Philosophy, Vol. III.* New York: Macmillan Publishing Co. and The Free Press, 1967.

Eicher, David J., ed. *Deep-Sky Observing with Small Telescopes.* Hillsdale, N.J.: Enslow Publishers, Inc., 1989.

Ford, Alice. *Edward Hicks: His Life and Art.* New York: Abbeville Press, 1985.

Frankl, Viktor. *Man's Search for Meaning: An Introduction to Logotherapy.* New York: Simon and Shuster, 1963.

Frommer, Arthur. *Europe on Five Dollars a Day.* New York: Simon and Shuster, 1969.

Griffiths, Bede. *The Marriage of East and West.* Springfield, Il.: Templegate Publishers, 1982.

Hammacher, A.M. *Vincent van Gogh: Genius and Disaster.* New York: Abradale Press, 1985.

Happold, F.C. *Prayer and Meditation: Their Nature and Practice*. Baltimore: Penguin Books, 1971.

Harrington, Philip S. *Touring the Universe with Binoculars: A Complete Astronomer's Guidebook*. New York: John Wiley and Sons, Inc., 1990.

Holy Bible: King James Version. London: Oxford University Press.

Jerusalem Bible. Garden City, N.Y.: Doubleday and Company, Inc., 1966.

Klausner, Neal and Kuntz, Paul G. *Philosophy: The Study of Alternative Beliefs*. New York: The Macmillan Co., 1961.

Kohak, Erazim. *The Embers and the Stars: A Philosophical Inquiry into the Moral Sense of Nature*. Chicago: University of Chicago Press, 1984.

Levy, David H. *Sky-Watching*. Sydney: Weldon Owen Pty, Ltd., 1994.

Lewis, C.S. *Perelandra*. New York: The Macmillan Co., 1944.

——————. "Religion: Reality or Substitute," *Christian Reflections*. Grand Rapids, Mi.: William B. Eerdmans Publishing Co., 1968.

——————. *The Screwtape Letters*. New York, The Macmillan Company, 1961.

_____. *Surprised by Joy.* New York: Harcourt, Brace and World, 1955.

_____. "Transposition," *The Weight of Glory and Other Addresses.* Grand Rapids, Mi.: William B. Eerdmans Publishing Co., 1965.

_____. *The Voyage of the Dawn Treader.* New York: The Macmillan Co., 1954.

Niebuhr, Reinhold. *The Nature and Destiny of Man.* New York: Charles Scribner's Sons, 1941.

New American Bible. Camden, N.J.: Thomas Nelson, Inc., 1970.

Norton, Arthur P. and Inglis, J. Gall. *Norton's Star Atlas and Telescopic Handbook.* London: Gall and Inglis,1959.

Novalis. *Hymns to the Night.* Sussex, U.K.: Clairview Books, 1992.

Noyes, Alfred. *Collected Poems.* New York: Frederick A. Stokes Co., 1913.

Pegis, Anton, ed. *Introduction to Saint Thomas Aquinas.* New York: Random House, 1948.

Pierce, Ida A. *Home Poems.* Rehoboth, Ma.: Isaac Chase and Son, Printers, 1910.

Progroff, Ira, trans. *The Cloud of Unknowing.* New York: Dell
    Publishing, 1957.

Rahner, Karl, S.J. *On the Theology of Death.* New York: Herder
    and Herder, 1961.

Shaara, Michael. *The Killer Angels.* New York, Random House,
    1974.

Sheehan, William. *The Immortal Fire Within: The Life and
    Work of Edward Emerson Barnard.* Cambridge, U.K.:
    Cambridge University Press, 1995.

Smith, Huston. *The Religions of Man.* New York, Harper and
    Row, 1958.

Suzuki, Shunryu. *Zen Mind, Beginner's Mind.* New York:
    Weatherhill, 1987.

Tolkien, J.R.R. *The Fellowship of the Ring.* Boston: Houghton
    Mifflin Co., 1982.

Trefil, James. "Was the Universe Designed for Life?" *Astronomy,*
    Vol. 25, No. 6, June, 1997.

Updike, John. *Collected Poems, 1953-1993.* New York: Knopf
    Doubleday Publishing Group, 1993.

Zaehner, R. C., trans. *Hindu Scriptures.* London: J. M. Dent
    and Sons, Ltd., 1966.